THE CHANGING [

Wolvercote

with Wytham and Godstow

Ann Spokes Symonds

Ann Spokes Symonds

Robert Boyd
PUBLICATIONS

Published by
Robert Boyd Publications
260 Colwell Drive
Witney, Oxfordshire OX8 7LW

First published 1997

ISBN 1 899536 13 2

OTHER TITLES IN THE

CHANGING FACES SERIES

Botley and North Hinksey
Cowley
Cowley: Book Two
Cumnor and Appleton with Farmoor and Eaton
Headington: Book One
Headington: Book Two
Jericho
Littlemore and Sandford
Marston: Book One
Marston: Book Two
Summertown and Cutteslowe
Woodstock

Anyone can publish a book — why not you!

Have you ever wanted to publish a book? It is not as difficult as you might think. The publisher of this book provides a service to individuals and organisations large and small.

Advise can be given on all facets of production: typesetting, layout and design, paper stocks, styles of binding including wired, perfect, sewn, limp and cased binding, the options are almost endless. If you have a project you would like to discuss why not contact:

Robert Boyd
PRINTING & PUBLISHING SERVICES
260 Colwell Drive
Witney, Oxfordshire OX8 7LW

Printed and bound in Great Britain at The Alden Press, Oxford

Contents

Cover illustrations

Front: The start of a ladies' outing in the 1920s outside the White
         Hart, Wolvercote.

Back: The centre of Wytham in about 1910 (D. Wilson collection).
         The Trout Inn, Godstow in 1997.

Acknowledgements

This book could not have come about without the help of numerous people from Wolvercote, Wytham, Godstow and Oxford who lent me photographs, shared their memories with me, identified people and verified facts. I am exceedingly grateful to them all for the time and trouble they took. I wish to thank: Mr and Mrs Ron Bateman, Mr Gerald Collett, Mrs G. Collett, Mr Leslie Collett, Mrs Vera Couch, Mr and Mrs C. Dale, Mrs Kathy Day, Mr Tim del Nevo, Mr F. L. Drewett, Mrs Jessie Dunkley, Mr Keith Duncan, Mr Peter Foden, (Oxford University Press), Mr and Mrs Stephen Franks, Mrs Val Faulkner, Mrs Nellie Giles, Mrs Peggy Godwin, Dr Malcolm Graham (Centre for Oxfordshire Studies), Dr Frances Gotch, Mrs R. Green, Miss Jasmine Howse (Wolvercote Local History Society Archivist) The Hon. Mrs M. Hadfield, Mrs Janacek, Jeremy's Postcards, Mr John Kempson, Ms N. la Vertue (Oxfrordshire Photographic Archive), Mrs Frances Lambert, Miss Ethel Lavis, Mrs Janet Ledger, Mr Mike Ledger (Wolvercote Local History Society Pictorial Archivist), Mr Fred Loveridge, Mrs Beulah Loveridge, Mrs Sheila Hoey Middleton, Mr Mundy, Mrs K. Ody, Mr Len Oakes, Mrs Osborn-King, *Oxford Mail and Times* Library staff and Mr Keith Price (Picture Editor), Mr Harry Rathband, Mr and Mrs Michael Stewart, Mr W. Soanes, Mr Peter Stone, Mrs Joan and Mr Ian Taylor, Mr Percy Tollett, Mrs Ruth Thomas, Mr and Mrs Ray Venney, Mr David Wilson and Mr Peter Wright. I should also like to thank my husband Richard for his help and encouragement and Dr Desmond Walshaw for his indispensable computer skills.

NOTE RE THE PHOTOGRAPHS

As others have found when working on issues in this series, one of the most difficult decisions is what photographs to include and what to discard. Some of the original photographs were faded or unsharp and did not reproduce well but I have included a few for historical reasons or to illustrate a point. I hope that readers will therefore forgive the quality in order that they can at least gain some impression and be able to appreciate the atmosphere of the old place or event.

Wolvercote

In the Domesday book the village was known as Ulfgarcote, taking its name from Ulfgar the Saxon, who had a cottage or homestead there, but by 1135 the name 'Wolvercote' had come into being.

Situated on the edge of the wide expanse of Common and the open stretches of Port Meadow, the inhabitants have always jealously guarded their rights and strongly defended their open spaces against the repeated efforts of the City to enclose or develop the land to serve Oxford's growing population. Peter Snow in his *Oxford Observed* says: 'The Meadow is to Wolvercote what the sea is to a tiny seaport, a broad horizon encompassing and dominating the community at every turn.' Roger Green, the Wolvercote poet, describes it as a 'border-line case — a place neither City nor country, nor suburb ... a place where buses pause before turning round' and also 'where the locals can afford to be friendly to strangers, knowing that tourism will never trouble them.'

Wolvercote's location about three miles from the City also accounts for its place in national history. Elizabeth I came through the village on both her visits to Oxford in 1566 and 1592, travelling south on her way back to London. At the time of the Civil War, Charles I established his headquarters in Oxford and during the seige required fodder for his horses. He made a written agreement with tenants of land at Wolvercote and 61 freemen to provide hay for the King's stables. Royalist troops were billeted in the village and one of its two mills was used by the King's armourers to grind sword blades. In the Spring of 1664, when King Charles escaped from Oxford by night, he and his 3,000 men took the unguarded track across Port Meadow to Wolvercote and Yarnton and Bladon to the north.

Queen Elizabeth I. (Oxford Hist. Portrait Exhibition, 1904.

Dominant over the village is the paper mill. The river, necessary for its function, has also played an important part in the life of Wolvercote. On a Summer afternoon in 1862, Charles Dodgson (otherwise known as Lewis Carroll) and his friend Duckworth, Alice Liddell and her sisters, came by in a rowing boat. Dodgson then began to tell the children a story: that was the start of *Alice in Wonderland.*

Described in 1817 as a 'rather extensive village', Wolvercote was never a place of wealth, with most of its inhabitants living in simple hovels or earth-floored cottages, none of which survive. There was wholesale destruction of the old houses from about 1936. Nevertheless, a few fine houses from earlier centuries remain, such as Manor Farm, Church Farm House and Nunnery Close, though most have been altered by restoration. Much of the village is now a Conservation Area. In the 19th and 20th centuries came extensive development and all Wolvercote became part of the City in 1928/9.

The original low-lying village, which was subject to winter flooding, grew up around the mill at the edge of the Common. On higher ground to the east were built the Church, the School and some larger houses. The two settlements, Upper and Lower, have existed since the 16th century. The area known as Upper Wolvercote, but traditionally and informally 'upstreet' to older residents, is now separated from the rest by the canal and railway line. The built-up higher area has no visible boundary between it and neighbouring Summertown in the north of Oxford and most of its population has as its main focus the City rather than the village. The Ecclesiatical parish stretches across to Cutteslowe and the Templar road Estate on the east side of Banbury road. Although in previous centuries there was much rivalry between the two sides of the village, the fact that there is little rift today may be partly attributed to the Village Hall which acts as a focal point for the two parts and helps to nurture a sense of community. The Wolvercote Commoners, who took over the duties of the old Parish Council (which had been in existence since 1894) when Wolvercote became part of the City, also plays an important part in village life, holding two open meetings a year and conducting annual democratic elections. In more recent years the Upper Wolvercote Association was set up to keep an eye on the amenities of that area. Other organisations, such as the Women's Institute, Horticultural Society, Village Hall committee, Local History Society and St Peter's Players also bring all Wolvercote people together. Over the years there have been many organisations which have enriched village life, including the Royal British Legion, Scouts, Guides, Cubs and Brownies, Playgroups, Church groups, Pensioners, the Fish Good Neighbour Scheme, the Recycling Group and Wildlife Watch, to name a few.

The photograph on the opposite page is a view of Wolvercote from the air in the early 1970s. It shows the two railway lines and the expanse of Green and Common between Lower and Upper Wolvercote.

Below, the cover of the Parish Magazine which was used continuously in the 1960s and 1970s. Wytham came into Oxfordshire in 1973/4 and Wolvercote roads or flats which have come into existence since are: Bladon Close, Sheriff's Drive, Millway Close, Dove House Close, Rawson Close, Rowland Close and Goose Green Close. The monthly periodical AMBIT, which was launched in January, 1976, replaced the Parish Magazine but it was still Church-orientated until 1995.

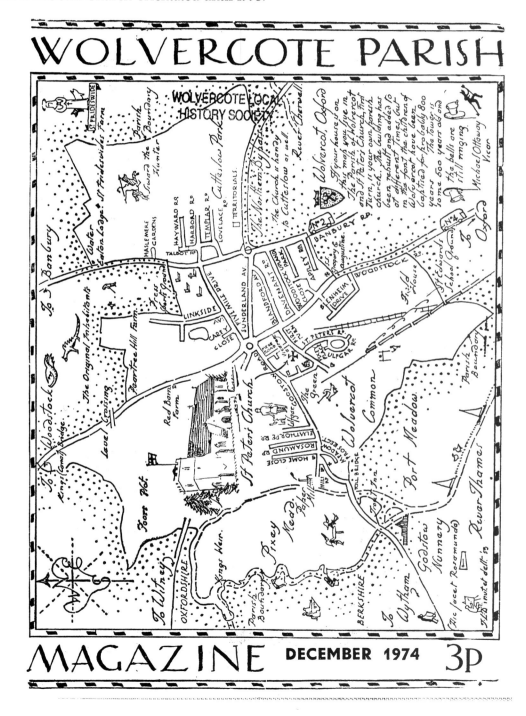

Farming

Katherine Rawson in 1706, left £200. for the purchase of lands for the use of the poor of this parish, after the payment of £1. per annum to the minister for preaching an annual sermon, and 10s. to the clerk. This charity now consists of 9 acres of meadow called the Poor's plat, which lets for £21. per annum, and after paying the sums named to the minister and clerk, the remainder is applied to the use of the poor and the National school. There is a lending library attached to the school.

Ball Howell, Esq.
Collingwood — Esq. Woolvercott fields
Gregory Thomas, Esq., New Cutslow
Lipscombe Mrs. Elizabeth
Middleton Mr. Henry, New Cutslow

Farmers.
Churchill Thomas
Dale James

Dean Joseph
Hedges Thomas
King William
Osborn Henry
Rowland John
William Richard

Miscellany.
Bustin Eliz., shopkeeper
Collett James, mason
Cox William, schoolmaster
Hedges Andrew, butcher

Keary William, shoemaker
Lipscomb William, vict., *Trout*, (& wine and spirit merchant) Godstow
Lock Mary, butter dealer
Quarterman William, baker
Round George, vict., *White Hart*
Rowland Edward, shopkeeper
Saxton Sarah, vict., *Red Lion*
Woodward John, vict., *Plough*
Wren Thomas, wheelwright

It can be seen from this 1852 entry in *Gardener's Gazzeteer* that there were eight farms in Wolvercote then. Life for many revolved round agriculture in those days. In the 1870s until about 1890 it was the custom to close school during the harvest and some children were taken away some weeks before breaking-up time to allow their mothers to work in the fields. Many children were granted leave of absence about March and April to help on the allotments and in September to assist with potato-picking. Boys were occasionally employed bird-scaring and sheep-minding. (Above the list of farms is a reference to the Rawson Charity which is still in existence.)

Every year there was a Fair on Alden's fields (where Home Close and Rosamund road are now). This large group was outside Alden's barn in about 1910—12 and it was probably taken on a Fair day. At the top of this barn in those days the boy scouts and cubs used to meet and they had to climb up a rather dangerous rickety staircase to reach it.

Fred Chamberlain, in his account of village life in Wolvercote in 1910, said the children who helped at haymaking in H.O. King's fields at Pixey Meadow were given the 'princely sum of sixpence per week'; hard work raking the hay in rows ready for the hay-forks because there were no mechanical elevators. At the end of a tiring day they were allowed to ride as far as the stables on the horses' backs. The hayricks, when completed, were covered with tarpaulin rick sheets. Joe Higgs made these in his large barn at the corner of Mere and Godstow roads for his employer, H.O. King. He tarred and stencilled the canvas sheets which were laid out on long tressles and then hung up on pulleys to dry. By 1929 there were only a hundred people working on the land and four owner-farmers supplied Oxford traders in a small way. A herd of cows owned by Mrs Revell, who lived in Wolvercote Green, were driven to the Meadow and back each day over the railway bridge until the 1960s.

Goose rearing once played a big part in the life of Wolvercote and is the reason why it is the village symbol. It was so much part of life that children were sometimes let off school. An entry in the school records of about 1929 states: 'Five boys and girls are granted leave of absence to mind the flocks of geese on Port Meadow as they sometimes wander into private grounds.' Before the days of vigilant school attendance officers, tending and finding geese was something many generations of Wolvercote children did at times when they should have been studying. As many as 200 geese were on Goose Green and 600 on the meadow. They did not mix but stayed in individual groups according to which family in the village owned them. They would make a clamour, especially if a fox came near, and those who owned them believed they were better than any watch dog or alarm system. It is no wonder that Wolvercote people were referred to as 'Gollins', a local rendering of goslings. The village was often styled 'Ganderland' by people who lived in Oxford or neighbouring villages. It was also said that everyone in the village had 'webbed feet.'

Geese at the edge of the stream near Toll Bridge, Wolvercote, 1996.

Wolvercote Women's Institute members with their new banner, depicting a goose girl and geese, in 1955. The Institute had been founded in 1918 and the first banner had worn out. Left to right: Mrs Chaplin (partly hidden), Mrs Frewin, Mrs Diddams, Mrs Catchpole, Mrs Slaughter, Mrs England, Mrs Spickernell, Mrs Hutchings, Mrs Stay, Mrs Wilson and Miss Woods. The banner is now displayed in a frame in the village hall.

Blacksmith Howell Saxton, known as 'Oakie' or 'Oke', a freeman of Oxford, (with beard), watching his son Ted shoeing a cart-horse. At first this took place on the forecourt of the Red Lion, the forge then being completely in the open air. From about 1919 onwards a new forge, with roof and walls (as here) was built at the back of the pub in Mill road. It was a favourite place for children to congregate, especially on winter evenings when they would edge as close as they could to the warmth of the forge. Fred Chamberlain has told how the blacksmith would often mend the children's iron hoops free of charge. Also, word soon got around if an unruly horse was being shod and might have to be put in a wooden frame while the shoes were being fitted. As a young boy, Leslie Collett told me that he used to wait in the blacksmith's yard from about 4 p.m. after school until his mother finished work at the mill opposite. He used to pull the rope to make the bellows go.

Unlike Wytham which has had a Lord of the Manor for centuries, Wolvercote has never been dominated by one large house or important family. This may account for the independence of its inhabitants and the reason they have been anxious to protect their rights. Nevertheless, it has had its champions in high places such as George Owen, Henry VIII's physician, who was Lord of the Manor, followed by his son and grandson, until in 1616 he sold the manor to Sir John Walter, Chief Baron of the Exchequer. David Walter, his son, helped the village freeholders to maintain their rights. In 1710, however, his descendants sold the manor of Wolvercote to the Duke of Marlborough and when a later duke sold most of the land in 1884, the manorial rights ceased. The Marlborough connection can be seen in some of the names of the roads: Blenheim, Blandford and Bladon. Although there was from then onwards no Lord of the Manor, there have nonetheless been people of influence and owners of land and property and one of these was Henry Osborn-King (1864–1946). Many people relied on him for their employment or as landlord of their homes. He was the son of Ann Osborn and William King, both of Wolvercote.

A few of the Osborn-King family in front of their home, Church Farm House, in about 1903—4.

Except for the addition of some windows, the place has not altered very much in the intervening years as this photograph of the house and its present occupants, taken in February 1997, shows. Sarah and Stephen Franks are seen with their sons, (left to right) Archie, Fergus and Henry, with their bicycles.

Henry Osborn-King with his wife Amelia (née Mott) whom he married in 1884. They had ten children. In the pony and trap are (left to right) the estate carpenter, H.O.King, Amelia King, their granddaughter and their daughter Ethel (born 1890).

H.O. King was much respected but also feared and it is said that 'he liked to get his own way.' He was a practical, shrewd and hard-headed man of businesss but still had time for public work. He became a member of the Parish and District Councils and was a Poor Law Guardian. He was a good musician and it is said that the tune *Wolvercote*, to which is sung the hymn 'Jesus I have promised', was his work. He was a loyal churchman, holding the office of churchwarden for many years and he had a pew in the church marked 'H.O. King and Family.' However, he often fell out with the Vicar about the music, complaining about the type of tunes and chants used. Fred Chamberlain in his *Remiscences of Wolvercote in 1910,* includes the following doggerel made up by some of the young choir members.

> *An egoist, deeply thinking, on his countenance a scowl,*
> *Deems our Sunday warbling like the screeching of an owl;*
> *Fitzherbert* [a chant] *has been banished and many another thing*
> *And chants and tunes and hymns are changed to suit old H. O. King.*

Health

Wolvercote doctors over the years included Dr Taylor, Dr Wink, Dr Bourne, Dr Hoey and Dr Hayden. Dr Wood (of Oxford) was the Foresters' (Friendly Society) medical man.

Dr Trevor Hoey seen here with his daughter, now Sheila Middleton Hoey, in the pram, and Sammy the dog, in the early 1940s. The inset picture shows him standing by his Vauxhall car in the 1930s. Dr Hoey, who was much-respected, took over the practice on the death of Dr Bourne in about 1935. Dr Hayden took over from Dr Hoey.

Dr Bourne was, apparently, quite a character. In the 1920s and 1930s when the children had whooping cough, he told them to go onto the Meadow near where the cows had been and that this would cure their coughs more quickly. This seemed to work, according to Beulah Loveridge and Nellie Giles who were around at the time. The top of the cow pats would be stirred with a stick and the odour sniffed. One little girl who had asthma was also advised: 'Go on the Meadow where the cows have been.' Dr Bourne did his own prescribing and would give the children grey pills in a matchbox. Harry Rathband told me that Dr Bourne took his first tooth out.

In the 1890s, the Sarah Acland Home (in Oxford) undertook nursing so long as subscriptions could be raised to pay the £30 or so required. Mrs Thompson was a local midwife who also laid out the dead. Mrs Godwin said: 'She would go to a birth one minute and a death the next.'

In 1900 a health statistician declared Wolvercote among the healthiest villages in Oxfordshire, being on low ground and not exposed to the cold north-east winds. The Wolvercote Infant Welfare Clinic in the village hall ran for many years until 1995. During 1965, for instance, 34 new babies attended. Volunteers from nearby suburbs came to help there.

Wolvercote Surgery, built in the early 1950s by Dr Hayden, with his own money, on Common land for which the Commoners gave permission. Before that, a surgery had been held at 105 Godstow Road. Dr Cartwright, who has been Wolvercote's doctor since about 1970, runs this surgery today. The photograph was taken in April 1997.

Transport

The Canal

It was the cutting of the canal in about 1778 (some half-century before the railways came), near the edge of the Meadow, which cut Wolvercote in two and emphasised more than ever its two parts of Lower and Upper. Early benefits of the canal included the conveyance of cheap coal (the Paper mill had its own coal barges), flour from Osney, cement, bricks for the brickyard and stones (later to be broken up for road-making). Today the canal serves no commercial purpose except the tourist industry. However, there are many narrow-boats moored for much of the length of the canal through Wolvercote. Some of these are those of visitors but others are in residential moorings allocated by British Waterways. A walk along the canal is an enjoyable pursuit and an interesting one. Each boat is different, some painted in traditional colours and some with small windmills which generate electricity.

A resident in her narrow-boat feeding her baby, taken in the late summer of 1996.

Railways

Criss-crossed by railway lines, it would be difficult to spend long in Wolvercote without seeing or hearing a train. The main Great Western Railway line from Paddington through Oxford to Worcester, Hereford and the Midlands, which also takes services from the North to the South coast, cuts the village in two. The old LMS line ran through Upper Wolvercote and the LNWR, running between Bicester and Oxford, stopped south of the bridge in First Turn. People could catch the train here — there were walkways each side of the tunnel leading to a small platform — and pay their penny fare on the train and be put down at Hayfield Road or Oxford.

The photograph shows one of the first trains to have no locomotive passing the halt near First Turn. Mr Edmund Cox (father of Beulah Loveridge) was a passenger guard at Oxford station. His wife Esther used to take a hot dinner in a container to this halt every day and it would be taken on the train from there to the station.

Wolvercote Halt on the GWR was just north of the railway bridge on Godstow road and its booking office was on the platform there. Both halts were opened in 1905 and closed in 1926.

This photograph shows the signal box and level crossing at Wolvercote Green in the 1950s.

6998 Burton Agnes Hall, one of the last steam trains, passing by the crossing on 3rd January, 1966. It was the 10.55 a.m. from Bournemouth to York via Oxford.

There was a great dispute with Britsh Rail concerning the closure of this crossing and the matter was debated in Oxford City Council. It was a useful access to the Meadow and had always been a right of way long before the railways came. When coal was collected from barges on the canal the man in the signal box would open the big swinging gates to let the carriers and their horses through. It was much resented by local people when the crossing closed and the signal box demolished and people still continued to cross over the line at this point despite a notice telling them not to. Mrs. Couch tells me that when she was a child a train just stopped in time as she was crossing and she got a 'terrible ticking off.' Now the trains no longer even blow a warning whistle as they speed past.

Winston Churchill came on his last journey to Bladon through Wolvercote in 1965 and many people waved from the Meadow or the bridge as the train taking his coffin came by.

Buildings

Villagers outside the White Hart Inn in about 1910. It is one of Wolvercote's three surviving pubs and the earliest. Although there has been an inn on the site since the mid-17th century, it has been known by other names.

On the right is Albert Young, with his horse and cart, and on the left Charlie Cross's carrier van. They were among a group of carriers who would take orders for purchases and bring them back from Oxford. Others were the Traffords, Joe White and Mr Hastings. A favourite story concerns Charlie Cross taking an order for women's 'drawers' and asking for 'breeches' at Cape's, the famous Oxford store. 'What size Mr Cross?', asked the blushing assistant. 'Well. hold them up and I will tell you', he replied. It was also said of Charlie Cross that his horse would bring him back home after his visits to town. Up until 1913 the only transport into Oxford was by horsedrawn carriers' carts or by train from the halt near the railway bridge in what is now First Turn. However, many would go on foot either by the canal path or, in summer, by Port Meadow. In 1902, a horse-drawn tram ran from South Parade, Summertown to Oxford.

On the far right of the picture, at the door of their cottage, are Mr and Mrs Chamberlain with (babe in arms) Olive.

The White Hart as it is today. (Courtesy Mike Ledger.) Note that the houses to the left of the pub have been replaced by a large paper mill building.

The Red Lion pub as it was in about 1910 when Mrs Rose Weston was the licensee. (Copyright Jeremy's postcards.) It has been in existence since the 18th century and was taken over by William Sexton (the name was later changed to Saxton) in 1814, together with the adjoining farrier's shop. (This and further useful information on Wolvercote pubs can be found in Mike Gotch's article in *Wolvercote Papers Number Two* published by the Wolvercote Local History Society.)

The Red Lion in November 1996. Note the new extension to the left and the paper mill buildings on the right.

The Plough at the edge of Wolvercote Green, with views over the Meadow, in 1997. Especially popular with fishermen, it is owned by Morrells' Brewery and has been in existence since at least 1812.

The Brickworks, with its chimney, which were opened by the Oxford and Berkshire Brick Company on a site off Five Mile Drive in 1869. By 1871 they were producing 1½ million bricks a year, mainly for housing in Summertown and the east and west suburbs of Oxford. The builders, Kingerlee, who owned it for some years, closed it in about 1934. The clay was obtained from the pit which is now a lake off Linkside Avenue and Carey Close. A special kind of facing brick called sandstock was made and fired by three men who trod the mixture with their bare feet. In 1871 it was recorded that boys worked at the brickfield in spring and summer, returning to school for the autumn and winter terms. The photograph dates from about 1890.

Lower Wolvercote in 1910.

The same view in 1996. The thatched cottage and one house on the left have been demolished.

Joe White's house on the green road to Yarnton with Joe White (centre) in his garden. The house is no longer there and the site is now thickly wooded and fenced off. The name Joe White's Lane survives although it is sometimes called Nicholl's Lane.

Wolvercote Green in about 1917 before the Village Hall was built. (Courtesy of Jeremy's postcards.) Wolvercote Women's Institute did much to ensure the establishment of this vital village amenity. In a declaration of intent in 1929 they stated: 'the future is for the young and the older ones must learn to appreciate their aspirations and see that they have all the chances possible and for this end we seek to erect a Village Hall and club room.' Enough money was raised for the building to be opened in 1932. An infant welfare clinic was one of the important activities which took place there. In the summer of 1939, gas masks were distributed from the hall. During the war, the suitably named Mr Hall of the Service Welfare Society, who had 250 men under the rank of corporal on his books, organised dances three times a week with the help of volunteers. A war-time canteen was also held and during the time of Dunkirk, when soldiers were camped on Port Meadow, it was open three days a week. In January, 1943 a school canteen was held there for evacuees as well as local children.

The Village Hall as it is today. There is a Village Hall Committee of volunteers and the place is a hive of activity with bookings nearly every day of the year. A Montessori school is held there during the day on weekdays.

Highbury Stables in Godstow Road, the home of the Allen family, taken in about 1935. The boy on the right is John Allen (born 1926) and his friend Jo Williamson. The house dates from the 17th—18th C and is listed as a Grade II building.

The same house as it is today. Note the extra dormer window in the roof and the large extension on the right. (Both views taken from the north.)

Rosamund Road under construction in 1933–1934.

Tudor Farm, at the corner of Godstow Road and Mere Road taken in 1944 (P. S. Spokes). It was demolished in about 1951.

In the place of Tudor Farm are the three large blocks of Millway Close, taken in 1997.

Shops

Before the First World War, most villagers obtained all their provisions locally. William Chamberlain made and repaired shoes. Bread and cakes were available from Richard (Dicky) Rowland, the baker, at 101 Godstow Road. People would also take their home-made pies there to be baked. Fred Hastings had a slaughterhouse and butcher's shop in the village and his wife Fanny sold rice-pudding slices at a halfpenny a time. Many of the shops were just rooms in people's houses. Mr Arthur (Homer) Stone of 1 Cyprus Terrace, sold sweets and fishing-tackle. Choir boys, who were paid 2/6d — 3/6d a quarter, quickly spent it in this shop. Mrs Savings (Green Road) sold sweets; Stanley's (Green Road): bread, bacon and cheese; Mrs Simmons and Mr Freeman (Elmthorpe road): sweets, jam, sugar, rice and dried fruit; Mrs Hoblyn (corner of Elmthorpe): wool. Mr Cross cut hair and mended bicycles in the shop which later became Bravo's. Mr Leslie Collett remembers the bicycles upside down in the shop while people were shaved or had their hair cut. Fred Trafford (near the chapel) sold coal and it was also delivered by at least five others. W.W. Allen sold paraffin and cheese as well as coal. Gibson's (corner of Rosamund Road) supplied meat. Many goods were delivered to the door including, of course, milk. Mr Robinson, for instance, delivered milk and butter, Mr Hilsdon and 'Milky' Allen delivered milk, the latter in Upper Wolvercote. The milk float carried churns and people would measure it out in jugs. Thomas Gessey brought wet fish in a basket. Baker Lay of Jericho brought bread and cakes in a horse-drawn cart and the Oxford Co-operative Society delivered from their Summertown shop. Carlo's would come round with fish and chips. Even in 1965 Wolvercote contained 7 grocery shops, a butcher, hairdresser, 2 newsagents and a cycle shop. By 1997 there were less than six shops in the whole of Wolvercote.

Chamberlain's Stores, Mill Lane, in the 1950s. It was demolished in 1955 for an extension to the paper mill. Chamberlain, who became village postmaster in 1906 was said to be 'long in the head' and 'was as good as any lawyer when it came to understanding and sorting out problems relating to the Post Office.' (M. Cobb, *Wolvercote Recollections.*)

Godstow Road, right, leading into the village with the ground under water in the winter of 1990. (Courtesy Mike Ledger.) Note the Rowland Close flats in the distance.

The same view in 1997 which shows the houses built next to Wren's pond, giving a new view of Lower Wolvercote from the east.

Godstow Road looking north-west (from the car park) taken in 1969. On the left is the site of Webb's Close and on the right is Nunnery Close.

The same view showing Webb's Close on the left, taken in 1997.

Mrs Quartermain (in apron), the wife of a village baker, outside her house in Godstow Road in about 1905. She was the grandmother of Percy Tollett who, at the time of writing, still lives in Wolvercote. The house is the most eastern one in the row which includes the White Hart.

One of the remaining shops in Wolvercote, First Turn Stores, in St Peter's Road in 1997. It was built in the 1930s on the site of an orchard. Three other establishments, all in Godstow Road, are Robinson's Stores and Post Office, Smart's Take-Away Fish Bar, and G.M. Gillett, newsagent and confectionery. City Motors garage at Wolvercote roundabout also has a shop.

The Churches

St Peter's Church

There has been a church on the present site since at least early Norman times but the fact that the font is Saxon (and not brought from elsewhere) indicates that the history of the church is even older. From early times, until 1866, it was a chapel of ease to the mother church, St Peter's in the East in Oxford, and for many centuries it has been in the patronage of Merton College.

Until 1859 an attractive church of the perpendicular period (1377–1485) with a stone roof, stood on the site. The tower is practically all that remains. Inside the church, however, in addition to the font, there is the 17th C family tomb of the Walter family which includes the figure of Sir John Walter (d.1630), Chief Baron of the Exchequer, in his judge's robes, with his two wives, three daughters and three sons. A 13th C stone arch, all that is left of the beautiful north chapel, was retained above the tomb. One of the sons, David (d.1679), Lord of Wolvercote, who lived at Godstow, became High Sheriff of Oxfordshire and Groom of the Bedchamber to Charles II. He is commemorated by a bust high up on the north wall. In September 1644, during the Civil War, a large group of rebels from Banbury forced their way into the church in an effort to kidnap a 'gentleman of quality' but a man, with only a pair of gloves as a weapon, made them kneel and their only prisoner was the Duke of York's 'dwarf'.

In 1859, instead of undertaking necessary repairs, most of the church was ruthlessly destroyed. Sensibly, it was decided to retain the 15th C tower which gives some character to the Victorian building. The choice of architect (Charles Buckeridge) was also fortunate because he designed the new church in the 14th C style in keeping with the tower.

The east window contains some good quality Victorian glass. A sundial on the tower has the inscription Redeem the Time. Among those who contributed to the new church, the largest sum was from Thomas Combe (see the section on the Paper Mill) who gave £520, said to be for the new porch.

South-east view of Wolvercote Church in 1828 by J. Buckler. (Copyright Bodleian Library, Oxford. M.S. Top Oxon. a69, No. 602.)

The church in the early 19th C from an 1840 publication.

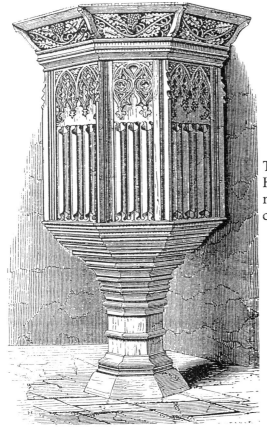

The pulpit, which dated from the time of Henry VIII, drawn in about 1830-40. It did not survive the demolition of the old church.

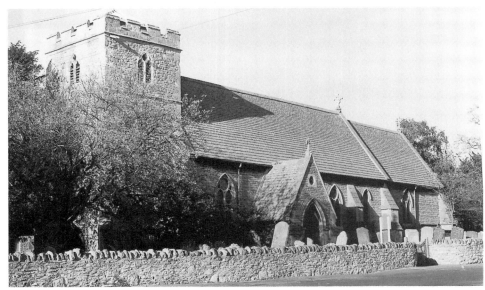

The church as it is today (1996). (Courtesy of Mike Ledger.)

In 1976, the Parish was united with St Michael's, Summertown and since 1982, Wolvercote has been part of the Ecumenical Parish of Wolvercote with Summertown.

The Roman Catholic church of St Gregory and St Augustine is to the south in the Woodstock Road.

The interior of St Peter's church in about 1909. At this time a ladder about ten feet high led from the ground to the loft where the bellows were operated by hand, The choir boys took it in turn to pump the handle up and down to keep up a sufficient supply of wind. The organ has since been moved to the back of the church. Note the curtain on the right, which was for keeping the draught out when the door was open, and the paraffin oil lamps hanging from above. The oil was carried in five-gallon drums from Chamberlain's stores in Mill Road to the church by two boys.

A Sunday School class in the Wolvercote Church Room in the late 1950s. Mrs Violet Smith is on the left.

Wolvercote choir boys in the 1950s. There has been a choir at St Peter's for centuries. On one occasion in the 19th century, it is said that on an outing to London several of the choir boys became separated from the main party and, seeing a policeman naively asked him if he knew the way to Wolvercote. Surprisingly, they were in luck because by pure chance the policeman said, 'Oh yes, Wolvercote. I come from there!'

Left to right: Ken White, E. Howard, Frank Cooper, W. Long, Geoffrey Tipton, Ivor Gurney.

The old church bells of St Peter's go for recasting, 1956. Left to right: Norman Chamberlain, Wilf Godwin, a representative of the bell founders, Taylor's of Loughborough. The church has had bells for over two centuries. From time to time the running gear or framework holding them has to be repaired and the bells recast.

Bellringers practising in February 1993. The Saxon font, seen here also, has witnessed the baptism of Wolvercote babies for at least ten centuries.

The dedication of the Bellamy Memorial Window, St Peter's Day 1976. It was designed by John Piper and made by Patrick Reyntiens.

Left to right: The Bishop of Dorchester, Mr John Piper, the Reverend Michael Ottaway (Vicar) and Michael Stockford (Churchwarden).

The Vicar of St Peter's, the Reverend David Michaels, shaking hands with Mr Jork Bugingo (a former member of the Church District Council) after morning service in February 1997. Looking on is Mr Michael Stockford, former Churchwarden.

The Baptist Church

Although the Baptist Church in Wolvercote was not built until 1886 a Baptist Meeting House had been licensed in 1672. This was housed in the home of James Beckford. In 1816 another licensed meeting place was set up in the home of John Ladson (later Nunnery Close). As a result of a lively 'Home Mission' undertaken by members of the New Road Baptist Church in Oxford some open-air meetings were held on the green in the lower village in 1884. One of those who attended was Daniel Collett, grandson of James, who had married Mary Ladson. There was such a good response that the Baptists outgrew a room belonging to Mr Norris (now 150 Godstow Road) and in 1884 started to meet in a barn belonging to Councillor G.H. Cooper who farmed from Bedford House in Godstow Road. Plans for a completely new building were begun in the spring of 1884, a site was given by Councillor R.J. Grubb and the cost of the buildings and furniture, estimated at £400, was met from donations. The architect was Frank Martin and the builder S. Hutchins of Kingston Road whose tender of £345 was the lowest. On 19th June 1886, six foundation stones were laid, including one by the then Mayor, Robert Buckell (later Sir Robert) who was a Baptist. By 1888 there was such a large Sunday school that extensions were necessary. The church owes much to its first superintendent, Mr Ernest Alden. He was a master butcher and a talented musician, playing the organ as well as preaching and conducting plays.

Many old Wolvercote families are found on the church roll. In 1913 the Sunday school was attended by 129 children and had 13 teachers. In 1929 there were further extensions to the hall and a kitchen added. During the Second World War the church hall was used for school actitivities additional to those at Wolvercote school. Over the years there have been active Women's and Young People's Fellowships, senior and junior choirs and a playgroup.

(More about the church can be found in *The History of Wolvercote Baptist Church 1884-1994* by J.E. Morgan-Wynne, 1985, and A History of Wolvercote Baptist Church by Gerald Collett, an article in *Wolvercote Papers Number One* published by the Wolvercote Local History Society, 1992.)

A boundary stone on the Common near Nunnery Close photographed in 1997. Sir Robert Buckell who was involved in the opening of the Baptist Church, was Leader of the Liberals in Oxford and Mayor 5 times. The date on the stone, 1886, was one of the times he was Mayor. He died in 1925.

The Baptist Church Girls' Choir during the First World War, taken in Alden's Field. The man is Mr Basil Collett and Sally Allen (organist) is sitting in front of him.

Interior of the church before 1910.

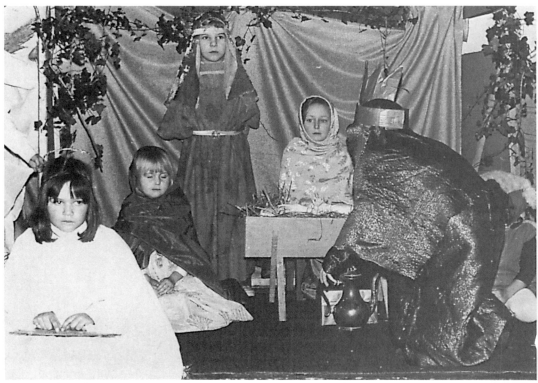

Baptist church Junior Youth Club Nativity play, 1971. Left to right: Clare Thornet, Nicola Collett, Andrew Tollett (Joseph), Tracy Mortimer.

The Baptist church at the time of the Flower Festival in 1984. (Courtesy Mrs Peggy Godwin.)

The Paper Mill

Paper has been made in Wolvercote since the middle of the 17th century but the Oxford University Press was the first-known user of Wolvercote paper for printing. From the start until about 1800 the paper was made by hand — a skilled occupation — but by the early 19th century the mill, being one of the leaders of the new processes, was making paper by machine.

In 1851, however, the mill was almost derelict with no machinery and no workers and if it had not been for Thomas Combe, Superintendent of the Clarendon Press and a partner in the Bible Press, it might never have survived. Combe, who was a great benefactor of both Wolvercote and the Pre-Raphaelite painters, saw the advantage of being able to make Bibles locally and cheaply and cut out the middleman. Known as the Patriarch, he bought the mill in 1855, rebuilt most of it and bought the Mill House as his home. He appointed John Stacy, a young engineer and capable manager, who was a man of ideas. He was also an amateur photographer and took this photograph of Thomas Combe and others in 1871.

Thomas Combe, the great benefactor of Wolvercote and the Arts, standing (right) with friends and colleagues. Back row (l to r): Prof. Bartholomew Price, Master of Pembroke College and Secretary to the Clarendon Press (1861-84); his sister, Mrs George; her son Hereford George, the first man to give lectures on geography in Oxford. Front row: Mary Beck, Miss Abbott and Miss Price. The photograph was taken outside the Mill House, Wolvercote in 1871 by J.H. Stacy, Controller of the Mill (1855-83). (Courtesy Carter: *Wolvercote Mill* and OCA.)

In 1857 Combe built a school room in the north side of Mill Street where evening classes were held for the mill workers until 1868. From about 1858 Wolvercote became the main supplier of paper to the University Press. The mill ran on water power, being well situated by a fast-running stream. It was not until 1943 that water power ceased but water was still needed for the process. In the days of water power, if there was no one working at the mill at the time, water used to seep out as far as Elmthorpe Road and, according to Margaret Cobb in her *Recollections of Wolvercote,* people would complain to the mill owners: 'Your water's in our kitchen.'

Despite the 1870 Education Act, which set the school-leaving age at 12, some children started work at the mill as early as 9. After the 1901 Factory Act, however, young people were only employed after they had left school. The hours worked were long and no eating or drinking was allowed on the premises. In 1910 adult men were working a 72-hour week in six twelve-hour shifts from 6 a.m. to 6 p.m. with only Sundays off.

By the mid-1920s, wood pulp had replaced rag papers. A new machine house was built in 1953–58 and new offices were erected on the site of Combe's school room and part of the walled garden of the Mill House. In 1962 the mill employed 307 people and produced 300 tons of paper a week. In 1965 it was the first paper mill in the world to be computer-controlled. There are some who say that it is the oldest working mill in the world. (See Harry Carter: *Wolvercote Mill* and Peter Foden in *Wolvercote Papers No. 2.*)

Although the Oxford University Press still own the site, the Mill itself now forms part of SAPPI EUROPE. In 1990, SAPPI (South Africa Pulp and Paper Industries) took over the mill from a Finnish paper group and it produces coated paper for the label and publishing markets.

Mill people helping with the hay making in Wolvercote. Joseph Castle (left) was Controller of the mill from 1883 to 1916. The three in the middle are John Stone and his wife and son. He was carter at the mill and one dark night in November 1908, when walking home after attending the horses, he missed his way and fell into a settling tank. He died from his injuries on 8th December 1908 at the age of 62. In accordance with the Factory Act of 1901 all accidents had to be recorded. The only other death (in 1924) was that of James Gammage who scratched his finger while opening a bag of lead and succumbed to septicaemia at the age of 28. On the far right of the photograph, which was taken in about 1890 and comes from H. Carter's *Wolvercote Mill* published by OUP, is Charles Morris, the colour mixer. The women, in their white aprons, which they also wore to work, were rag pickers at the mill.

The rag house, a design inspired by Thomas Combe, taken in the 1950s. It was pulled
down in the 1960s. The building was so-called because that is where the women sorted
the rags used in paper making. (Courtesy Thomas-Photos and OUP.)

Paper making in the 1950s. In the vat is china clay used in paper making. The paper is being shown for the benefit of the photographer. (Courtesy Thomas-Photos and OUP.)

Paper making in the 1950s. (Courtesy Thomas-Photos and OUP.)

Young women checking the paper for quality. Taken in the 1950s. (Courtesy Thomas-Photos and OUP.)

Packing paper for dispatch is Jimmy Higgins who worked at the paper mill all his life. (Courtesy Thomas-Photos and OUP.)

This is Annie Collett who was born in 1893 and died in 1977. In the period between 1840 and 1918, of the 1,074 surnames found in the parish registers (which have been transcribed by Mr Jack Scarr) 483 were Collett, some way ahead of Allen (with 246), Robinson (222) and Mitchell (217).

More people probably worked at the paper mill during this period than anywhere else and Annie was one of them. Soon after her son Leslie was born (in 1920), when she was 27 years old, she started working there and joined other village women who daily ascended the two flights of stairs of the rag house tower. Here they not only picked over the rags but sorted good paper into different grades. The two jobs went together and it was piece-work so that they were paid according to the amount done. She would, like most of the women at the mill, have worn a white apron and they usually took their own footstool and high stool to work. By the 1940s she was earning an average of £2 10s a week for working from 7.30 a.m. to 5.30 p.m. every week day and Saturday morning. It was a dirty job cutting off the buttons from the old clothes. Other materials were old canvas from ships' sails and even old hoses from the Fire Brigade. In earlier days the women took snuff to counteract the smell. No rags were used after 1952.

After 47 years doing that job Annie helped in the canteen until her eyes were too weak. All the cats used to follow her when she was a tea lady because she would never ignore their requests for milk. After that, she helped with the cleaning which she did well into her 80s. Annie's husband also worked at the mill.

The School

There have been schools in Wolvercote since 1815 and a so-called 'National School' was held in the glebe house, supported by subscriptions, in 1817. In 1831 a new girls' schoolroom was built and by 1833 there were 50 boys and 50 girls aged between 5 and 11 paying one and a half pence a week each. In 1855—56 a new school was built on glebe land west of the Church in what is now John's bookshop and before that a Deep Freeze. By 1859 the average attendance was 150. Because there was no playground the children played on the Green down the hill and were recalled to school by Mr Boult (master and cricket enthusiast) who blew his whistle from the school door. It is unlikely that a whistle could be heard today above the noise of the traffic. This school was enlarged in 1875 and again in 1891 and 1894. On the second occasion an appeal called 'Wolvercote School Enlargement Fund' was led by the Vicar.

In 1897 some land across the road to the south of the Church had been given by the Duke of Marlborough, enabling the new infants' school to be built there. It was officially opened by the Duchess of Marlborough on 11th May 1898. At the start there were 130 infants while the older children continued in the old school. Mrs Lucy Ellis, wife of the schoolmaster, was school mistress for the infants. Her assistant, Miss Dolly Wren, daughter of Mr Thomas Wren, village wheelwright and coffin maker, is still remembered by village residents. She was a well-loved accomplished and respected teacher. She has been described as 'a dear' and who, at Christmas-time would bring a pudding to school which was then cut up and wrapped for each child to take a piece home to parents. She also took apples to school from her garden in the autumn.

It was not unusual for infants to start school as early as 2½ years old. Beulah Loveridge, for instance, told me she started two days before her third birthday and Peggy Godwin remembers pushing her little brother of three in a folding pram to school.

In earlier days, though, things were a little different with children leaving school as early as 9 to work. They learnt parrot fashion and had a rap on the knuckles if they did not learn by rote. When it was a Church school the children paid a penny a week and it was said that the Head's salary was based on the results of the Bishop's prize. In 1876, for instance, the Parish magazine reported a saisfactory H.M. Inspector's report with 85% passing in reading, writing and arithmetic. However, it also stated: 'It is a pity that more had not qualified by atttendance as in this case the government grant would be larger.' These grants were first received by the school in 1866.

A second school having been erected next to the infants' school in 1912—13, with an extended playground, it was at last possible for all the children to be accommodated on one site.

When the boundaries changed in 1929 the school was taken over by Oxford City Council. A quotation from the Women's Institute Scrap Book for that year reads: 'May the children remember that though they now become young citizens of the finest City in England, yet they still belong to the sturdy, independent stock of Wolvercote.'

Two more classrooms were added in 1938, enabling 416 children to attend. From 1965, until the room was required for teaching, the school had in it a heated swimming pool. It is now a First School, under Oxfordshire County Council, taking children between 5 and 9 years but with a nursery class for the under 5s. The latest extension to the rear was built in 1996—97.

A group of mothers, some with babies, outside Wolvercote School. Reverend Walter D. Sargent, who is on the left in the second row, was Vicar between 1895 and 1901 and this was probably taken after 1897. (Courtesy of Oxfordshire Photographic Archive.)

Wolvercote Council School class in about 1916.

Wolvercote Council School Soccer team in 1928. Back row (l to r): ?, ?, Les Thompson (seated), Jeff Tipton, Mr William Fallows (Head), Albert Collett, Dan Collett (seated), ?, Alf Warmington. Front row: Doug Beesley, Jim Waine, Len Trafford.

Morris dancers who performed in the Wolvercote School concert on 17th December 1928. Left to right: William Loveridge, Leslie Thompson, Geoffery Tipton, ?, A(?) Warmington, D. Beesley.

Children from Wolvercote School who took part in the Oxford City Sports in 1928. On the left is Mr W. Fallows (Head) and (in front of him) Miss Huckins. On the right is Mrs Slaughter (back) and Miss Pratt, teachers. The group includes: Mabel Fathers, Hazel Hall, Nora Warmington, Phyllis Waine, Margaret Couling, Hilda Cooper, Moyra Holland, Rose Pettifer, Chris Collett, Kay Trafford, Reg Green, Ivor Gurney, Reg Hale, Les Thompson, Aubrey Collett, Margaret Thompson.

A class at Wolvercote School in about 1930. Back row (l to r): ?, ?, ?, Bill Cooper, Donald Morley, Aubrey Collett, ?, Doreen Pettifer, Graham Hale. Middle row: Ruby Lovegrove, ?, ?, ?, Bill Wain, ?, Ernest Saxton, Arthur Loveridge, Mary Drewett, Gladys Haskins, Eric Panting, Gerald Collett. Front row: ?, Barbara Thompson, Don Panting, Basil Moss, Hilda Parsons, Susie Bourne, John Tuffly, Barbara Gregory, Peter Brooks, John Allen.

A class at Wolvercote School in about 1931 with Miss Spencer (left) the class teacher. Back row (l to r): Margaret Bourne, Brian Holland, — Clements, ?, Joyce Smith, Joyce White, ?, Donald Bourne, ?, Bernard (Mick) French. Middle row: Joe Williamson, ?, Phyllis Paine, Dennis Collett, ?, ?, ?, Val Mapson, Ronald Williams, Betty Pratley. Front row: Margaret Wild (just behind), Ray Venney, ?, ?, Bert Drewett, Kitty Haskins, ?, Eileen Parsons, John Saxton, Barbara French, Phyllis Allen, Dennis Gregory, Tom Stanley.

Dennis Gregory, the curly-headed little boy (second from right in the front row) was tragically drowned trying to jump across Wolvercote lock (by Goose Green). He just did not make it and became caught under the gate. On his left is Thomas Stanley. Ray Venney last saw his best friend Dennis running past his house on Wolvercote Green saying: 'I'm at war with Stanley!'. The next thing he saw was Mr Gregory carrying his son home wrapped in a blanket. Dennis was only nine years old.

Mrs Slaughter's class at Wolvercote School taken in the early 1930s. Back row (l to r): Kenneth Freeman, ?, ?, Peggy Allen, Winnie Ball, Mollie Cook, Ivy Pettifer, Frances Walker, Evelyn Ward. Third row: Graham Hale, ?, ?, ?, ?, — Belcher, ?, — Pettifer, Mrs Slaughter. Second row: Winnie Cox, Joan Thompson, Janet Gurney, — Howard, ?, ?, ?. Front row: none identified.

Wolvercote School Seniors Football XI, 1935–36. Back row (l to r) Mr W. Fallows (Head), Bill Walker, Mr G. Robinson (teacher). Middle row: Dennis Collett, Brian Holland, Jim Pratley, Keith Howard, Mervyn Williams. Front row: Graham Hale, Bertie Drewett, Bert Clements (Captain), Bernard French, Harold Millard.

A class at Wolvercote School taken in about 1931. Back row (l to r) Olive Cooper, Flossy Axtell, Glenys Ody, Dolly Viner, Graham Clanfield, Billy Walker, Gleny Ward, Iris Mott. Middle row: Miss Huckins (teacher), Beryl Clanfield, Rene Collett, Dorothy Hands, Muriel Gordon, Doris Couling, Charlie Brown, George Pratt, Margaret Bidmead. Front row: Bert Clements, Jimmy Pratley, Jean Allen, Ron Williams, Nellie Loveridge, Beatrice Higgs, Barbara Merry, Joan Drewett, George Stone, Joyce Hastings, John Stone, Violet Carter.

Class V at Wolvercote Council School in about 1931 with Miss Huckins, (teacher) who married John Morton. Back row (l ro r): Tom Stanley, Ray Venney, Dennis Gregory, − ?, Peggy Wilde. 4th row: Miss Huckins, − ?, − ?, − ?, Don Bourne. 3rd row: Oliver Greenway, − ?, − ?, − ?, Val Mapson. 2nd row: Eileen Parsons, − ?, Phyllis Allen, Joyce White. Front row: Bernard French, − ?, Ken Herring. The girl holding the Class V notice is possibly Doreen Pettifer.

Wolvercote Council School Junior Football team, 1935–36 Back row (l to r) Mr A. Quarterman (teacher) and Mr W. Fallows (Head) Middle row: Peter Sharman, Howard Truss, Ernest Saxton, Bill Cooper, Tom Hill. Front row: A. Stevens, Gerald Collett, Graham Hale (Captain), Desmond Truss, Roy Collett.

This May Day photograph of 1941 or 1942 was of a group of children from Wolvercote School who attended 'over-flow' classes at the Baptist Church Hall. It was taken in about 1942. 1 Joan Aries, 2 Tina Hall, 3 Hazel Drewett, 4 Pat Alderman, 5 ?, 6 David Sparkes, 7 Betty Duffin, 8 ?, 9 Michael Warmington, 10 Clive Alderman, 11 Tony Hewlett, 12 Barbara Thompson, 13 ?, 14 Cynthia Edmonds, 15 Stewart Lock, 16 ?, 17 Judy Fidler, 18 ?, 19 ?, 20 ?, 21 Shirley Gibson, 22 ?, 23 Gloria Cheshire, 24 Shirley Gibson,   25 Jean Fisher, 26 Susan Freeman, 27 ?, 28 A. or B. Thompson, 29 ?, 30 ?, 31 Maureen Holihan, 32 John Truby, 33 ?, 34 ?, 35 George Freeman, 36 ?, 37 ?, 38 John Weaver,   39 Brian Lloyd, 40 Eileen Fisher, 41 ?, 42 Ken Hope, 43 Brian Cheshire, 44 John Mortimer, 45 Tony Mortimer.

A Nativity Play performed by Wolvercote School on 22nd December 1942. The group includes Susan Bradshaw, – Bell, Tony Revell, Margaret Chamberlain, Margaret Cornish and Jean Cornish.

A class at Wolvercote School taken in 1946–47. 1 Mr George Robinson (teacher), 2 Mr Bill Fallows (Headmaster), 3 Bill Crumley, 4 Monica Hilsdon, 5 Brian Collins, 6 Doug Portman, 7 Ann Murphy, 8 Pam Nicholls, 9 Mick Brown, 10 ?, 11 Yvonne Summersfield, 12 Barbara Lee, 13 ?, 14 ?, 15 Jean Harper, 16 John Nicholls, 17 John Duffin, 18 Lavinia Simms, 19 Stan Viner, 20 John Thomas, 21 Shiela Giles, 22 Brian Taylor, 23 Pearl Castle, 24 B. Savage, 25 Jill Pether, 26 Anne Tomlinson, 27 Mavis Mortimer, 28 Christine Newport, 29 ?, 30 Alan Savage, 31 John Beale, 32 Anne Jeaacock, 33 Brian Sutton, 34 David Sawyer, 35 Margaret Cornish, 36 Barbara Pitson.

The front of Wolvercote School in October 1966 (Courtesy of M. Ledger.)

The School from the west showing the south extension being built in November 1966.

Sports, Activities and Drama

Wolvercote has had a tradition of particpating sports for well over a century. The Cricket Club was already flourishing in the 1860s and in the 1890s the Church (St Peter's) even had its own cricket team. In August 1890 there was an amusing match between the ladies and gentlemen. The paper mill also had its own team for a while.

Wolvercote Cricket Club and supporters in 1913 when they won *The Daily Telegraph* Cup. Back row, (l to r): L. Puddiphat, Mr H.O. King, S.J. Ellis, D. Collett, The Rev E.A. Sydenham, H. Collett, B. Leach, A.F. Willoughby, S. Thompson. Middle row: V. Mathews, S.H. Collett, C.W. Warwick, Mr H.S. Kingerlee (President), A.D. Collett (Vice-Captain), A. Warmington, T. Beesley. Front row: O.O. Price (Hon. Secretary), B. Waine, W. Howard (Captain), B. Beesley, J.H. Woodward.

The Wolvercote Cricket Club team in 1962 when, as can be seen, they won *The Daily Telegraph* Cup for the second time. Back row (l to r): Keith Evans, Fred Drewett, Dennis Payne, Geoff Hibbins, Allan Waine, Mic Baughan. Front row: Ray Venney, John Duffin, David Walker, Doug Howes, John Simms, John Weaver.

Wolvercote Football Club in 1947—48 when they won the Charlbury Charity Cup. Back row (l to r): Doug Howes, Eric Inness, Bert Timms, John Saxton, Basil Collett, Graham Hale. Front row: Dick Holihan, Frank Williams, Alan Drewett, Roy Collett, Bert Clements.

A Football Club outing to Weymouth (taken in the early 1950s?). It includes Brian Rolls, J. Bowerman, Bill Giles, Bill Drewett, Bert Clements, Dennis Payne, George Tuckwell and Keith Evans.

Wolvercote Cycle Speedway about 1947. The track was between the allotments and what is now Rowland Close. Back row (l to r): Allen Waine, Roy Gascoigne (on cycle), Reg Viner, Tony Collins, John Gascoigne, Bill Waine, Arthur Prince (on cycle). Front row: Arthur Butler, Mick Rivers, Brian Neville, Mick Parker, Fred Drewett.

Wolvercote Sports Day, about 1946-'51) Seated (l to r): Back row: Mrs Matthews, (at table) Mrs N Martin (in white hat), wife of the Leader of Wolvercote Boys' Club, Mrs D.M.Rebbeck and the Rev. P. Rebbeck. Standing: Mr A.W.L. Compton (Headmaster, Wolvercote School) with Miss Spooner, daughter of the famous Dr Spooner. (Courtesy John Kempson.)

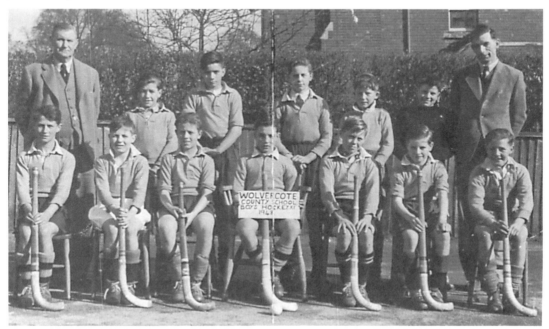

Wolvercote Boys' Hockey XI, Wolvercote County School, in 1948. Back row (l to r): Mr Bill Fallows (Head), A. Butler, B. Harper, R. Brockel. J. Gillett, R. Gregory, Mr Quarterman. Front row: D. Burgess, B. Mullins, M. Parker,, B. Prince, B. Smith, B. Prately, K. Plato.

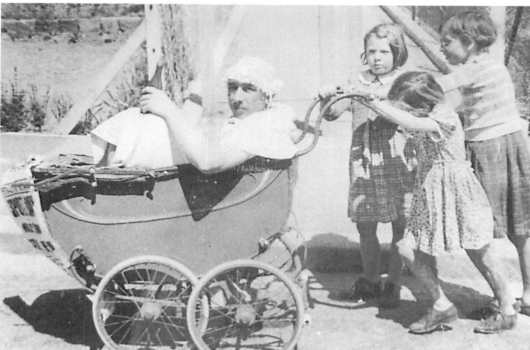

Wolvercote Sports Day, 2nd June, 1951. Top picture (l to r): A. Lewis, R. Foster, J. White, J. Pratley. Bottom: R. Walker (in pram), Brenda Clare, ? (face obscured), Linda Lewis.

Cricket Club on Wolvercote Common with some ladies who took part in the game, 1953. Back row (l to r): Mr Baughan, George French (in cap), Mick Potter, Peter Whitlock (in cap), Peter Walker, Jim Crozier, Alfie Collett (umpire), Mrs Baughan, Mick Baughan, Bert Clements, Roy Gascoigne (at rear), J. Duffin (in cap), Allen Ball. Middle row: ?, Nora Williams, ?, Mrs Whitlock, Dorothy French, Ann Truby, Mrs Simms, Betty Duffin, Lavinia Simms, Mrs Cornish. Front row: John Simms and Jean Cornish.

An Alan Course cartoon from the *Oxford Mail*, 1953, when Wolvercote Football team 'A' played Wolvercote 'B' team. The 'A' team won, which saved embarrassment.

Wolvercote Darts team outing in the early 1960s. Far back row (l to r): Jack Stockford, Frank Craddock. Back row: Harry Drewett, ?, Harry Hastings, (Landlord, White Hart), ?, Harold Griffin, ?, Frank Collett, ?, ?, ?, ?, ?. Front row: Stan Payne, ?, ?, ?, Harry Brockell (in front), Mr Hopkins, ?, Jimmy Quainton, Mr Knight (far right).

St Peter's Players

The Dramatic Society, which takes its name from the Church, was started in 1945 by Miss Joan Parker, (now Mrs Joan Taylor), a teacher at Wolvercote School, and the Reverend Thomas Lewis, Curate at St Peter's. With a nucleus of about ten people, all from Wolvercote, it put on plays (usually one-act) on a shoe-string throughout the war years. Their final performance was in 1945 which, was *Cinderella* written and produced by Miss Parker

In aid of the Wolvercote Welcome Home & Church Hall Fund.

ST. PETER'S
PLAYERS
PRESENT

A Grand Christmas Pantomime

CINDERELLA

CHILDREN'S MATINEE:
SATURDAY, JANUARY 5th,
The Village Hall, Wolvercote, at 2.30 p.m.

MONDAY, JANUARY 7th,
Summertown Memorial Hall, at 7.15 p.m.
(No children unless accompanied by adults).

THURSDAY, JANUARY 10th,
The Village Hall, Wolvercote, at 7.30 p.m.
(No children unless accompanied by adults).

BOOK
THESE
DATES

Also   THE PARISH SOCIAL
December 31st, 1945, The Village Hall, Wolvercote
at 7.30 p.m.
(No people under seventeen).

The poster for *Cinderella*.

Scene from *Pride and Prejudice,* about 1944. Left to right: Mrs Bennett (Joan Parker), Elizabeth (Doris Ensor), Mr Collins (The Reverend Arthur Adcock), Jane (Barbara Long), Lady Catherine de Bourgh (Margaret Heading).

There being no one willing to take over from Miss Parker, the Players ceased and were not restarted until 6th May, 1955. The then Vicar, the Reverend Michael Ottaway, became Chairman of the revived Players and Miss Glenys Palmer (later to become Mrs Ottaway) was Secretary and Treasurer. It has been in existence ever since, putting on regular performances at the Village Hall.

Some of the cast of Joseph Andrews by Henry Fielding, March 1983. Left to right: Alan Palmer, Peter Welply, Lucy Neale (now Mrs Norton).

The Boys' Club

During the Second World War a Community Centre was run by the City Council at Lower Farm in St Peter's Road and there were boys' and girls' clubs attached to it.The Boys' Club was officially founded in 1939. When the old farmhouse was demolished the present building was erected at a cost of £10,000 and officially opened by the Marchioness of Blandford on 30th October 1959. Girls were admitted in 1972. The Club has had a great influence on the life of young people in Wolvercote and good friends were made. Michael Stockford in a poem about the club written in 1985, 40 years on, remembers:

> *We played on the cut: 'Let's jump the lock',*
> *Fished for tiddlers, with an old sock,*
> *How innocent we were – had lots of fun*
> *Girls and boys we played as one.*

John Kempson, the present club leader, has been in the post since August 1969. The photograph shows him with a group of club members and holding the Wilkinson Sword Club Leader of the Year award in 1985. For becoming the national winner of the United Kingdom he won a holiday in the USA. Members include: Sean Reck, Adam Stanley, Trevor Nash, Ruth Kempson, Lara England, David England, Scott Venney, Jason Gardner, Fred Broughton, Justin Broughton, Nick Price, Jason Price, Mark Strong, Haydon Carter, Joanne Murdy (?), Alan Howard.

Dr Desmond Walshaw (left), for many years Hon. Treasurer of the Wolvercote Boys' Club, receiving the *Keystone* award from the Duke of Marlborough, President of the Oxfordshire Association of Boys' Clubs.

For his victory in the French Wars, a national award was made to the first Duke of Marlborough in the form of the Blenheim Estate and he thus became the owner of a large part of Wolvercote village. Other landowners at that time were Christ Church, Merton and St John's colleges and the Dashwood family.

The Pond. A Voluntary Project

Wolvercote Green with College Pool in the foreground as it was in January 1991. (Courtesy of Dr A.W. McDonald.)

As ponds have to be dug out every 25 years or so, this one was restored as a community project by a band of volunteers in 1990. A haven for wildlife, it is a popular amenity with young and old alike.

The Women's Institute

The Wolvercote Women's Institute was founded in 1918 with Lady Westland as it first President and Miss Grace Fletcher as its first Secretary. Over the years, among a host of different activities, it has taken part in pageants and put on its own plays and displays. It continues today to hold monthly evening meetings, with speakers, at Wolvercote Village Hall, a place they did so much to initiate. These photographs of W.I. events are courtesy of the Wolvercote Women's Institute archives.

A group of W.I. members who performed *A Midsummer Night's Dream* in about 1927. The house in the background was The Croft, which belonged to Alden's, the printers. (It was replaced by Sheriff's Drive.) The play took place at 'The Nook', to the east of Nunnery Close. Back row (left to right): Mrs Savage, Mrs Nevin, ?, Mrs Westbury, Mrs Allen. 3rd row: Mrs Freeman, Mrs Willis, Mrs E. Loveridge, Mrs Collett, Mrs Collett (later Mrs Robinson), Mrs F. Waine, Miss Slade, Mrs Cox, Mrs Jo Fathers. 2nd row: Mrs Hathaway, Miss Dumerique, Mrs Pettifer, ?, Mrs Marjorie Mott, Mrs S. Waine, Mrs Violet Smith, Mrs Robinson. Front row: Mrs F. French, Mrs Taylor, Nurse Hussell.

Outing to the British Empire Exhibition in 1924 or 1925. The group includes Miss Fletcher, Mrs Robinson, Mrs Taylor, Mrs Bessie Loveridge, Mrs Collett, Miss Rowland, Mrs Hutt, Mrs Brookes, Mrs Fathers.

Judges at a W.I. Produce Show tasting some of the entries. Taken in the late 1920's. Left to right: Mrs Fallows, Mrs Masters (Cooking judge) Mrs Willis and Miss Morris-Smith.

The Golden Jubilee of Wolvercote Women's Institute in 1968. A group of the longest-serving members. Back row (left to right): Miss E. McKibbon, Mrs Ponting, Mrs Thompson. Front row: Mrs E. Loveridge, Mrs H. Tollett, Mrs M. Venney (President, cutting the birthday cake), Mrs. V. Smith and Mrs M. Freeman. (Courtesy *Oxford Mail and Times.*)

The Institute meets every second Tuesday evening in the Village Hall. Following the business, they always have a speaker followed sometimes by a competition. Over the last few years, talks have been given on a wide variety of subjects, including Life in the Cabin by a British Airways crew member, Fashion Trends in Footwear, The British Red Cross, The Royal National Lifeboat Institution, Fifty Years of Nursing, a psychologist looking at human relationships, Animal Welfare, Beekeeping and Products of the Hive, The Other Side of the Footlights, Hearing Dogs for the Deaf, and The Work of Parliament by the local M.P. The Institute also has its own drama group.

The Wolvercote Local History Society

The society was established in 1987. It holds well-attended meetings about four times a year and in Summer often has a Midsummer Walk. This group of members and friends is listening to Mr Peter Stone (with book), a knowledgeable local resident, during a walk round Wolvercote in June, 1996. Included in the picture are Mrs E. Loft-Simson, Miss Christine Kennedy, Mrs V. Barnish, Mrs Burchardt, Lady (Sally) Baldwin, Dr Alison McDonald (with dog) and Miss Jasmine Howse (Local History Society archivist).

The society has published two booklets, Wolvercote Papers Number One in 1992 and Wolvercote Papers Number Two in 1996.

Wolvercote Events

The Battle of Wolvercote

Wolvercote folk, proud of their independence and always ready to defend their rights of common, were often in dispute with the City people. It is even claimed that if it had not been for the Commoners the City would have encroached further than they did onto Port Meadow. Since 1563, Wolvercote people had established rights of intercommoning for their animals and this, in turn, gave them an equal say with the Freemen about the Meadow's preservation.

In 1889 there was an extension of the Boundaries Act and the ditch which divided Meadow and common, which local people called 'our ditch', ceased to be in the parish of Wolvercote and was transferred to the City of Oxford. To make it official the City Engineer arranged for the boundary stone to be removed to the Wolvercote side of the ditch. So great was the anger and resentment of the villagers that they moved the stone back again. Next time, when the City used concrete to fix the stone, some children who had seen it being done, picked out the concrete before it dried. This enabled the Vicar, together with the Controller of the Paper Mill and some strong men of the village, to roll the stone back again.

It was on 17th August 1892, when the Mayor and Corporation 'came round the franchises' (beating the bounds), including the ditch, that trouble really started. Children, who had seen the procession arriving, ran to tell the Vicar, the Rev. F.W. Langton. He and a former curate, the Rev. Anthony Bathe, who was visiting him, both made for the ditch and as the Mayor and Corporation came to the stone, the Vicar read out a protest against the stone's removal. However, someone in the Mayor's party shouted 'Forward Oxford' and the band struck up *See the Conquering Hero Comes* and there was some armed combat between the two sides. Stones and earth flew about and Mr Bathe put up his umbrella to protect his silk hat. He was much annoyed that a report in Oxford later wrongly stated that he had used his umbrella as a weapon. One of the reasons why the ditch, and especially that part at the north near Nunnery Close, was claimed by the Commoners was that they had had sheep-washing rights in it for hundreds of years. There was, however, one consolation for the village; they no longer had to keep the ditch clean.

The contemporary photograph on the opposite page shows the crowds congregating near the ditch during the battle.

2,226 people subscribed to the plaque (above) which commemorates the deaths of Lieutenants Bettington and Hotchkiss, members of the Royal Flying Corps, who were killed when their aeroplane crashed just north of Toll Bridge on 10th September 1912. Inserted in the north side of the bridge, this is how it looked in 1997. Some of the wreckage of the plane can be seen below (Courtesy of Jeremy's Reproduction Postcards).

Toll Bridge takes its name from the tolls which people paid when there was a Fair in the neighbouring field. In 1142 Empress Matilda had granted the Fair to Godstow Abbey and one was held on every St John the Baptist's Day until about 1390. In recognition of the two airmen who died, the County Council in the 1970s renamed it 'Airman's Bridge', but most local people prefer its older historic name.

This photograph, taken on Port Meadow during the summer of 1917, shows a BE 2e aircraft with a young lady and her brother posing in front of it.

The Sheriff's Drive

Until 1835 Port Meadow was supervised by the City bailiffs but when a new officer called the Sheriff came into being it was he (for many years they were male) who became the Conservator of the Meadow. There had been 'drifts' or drives to control the pasturing since the 16th Century but in more recent times there has usually been one annual drive a year led by the Sheriff. The gates are closed the previous evening, to prevent any horses or cattle being removed, and at dawn the animals, now usually limited to cattle, are driven and herded into the pound which is a fenced-off part of the Meadow. Until the pound was built the animals were driven along the road as far as Godstow as in the photograph.

A civic party in the grounds of the Nunnery at Godstow with cattle which had been herded there after the Sheriff's Drive. In 1943, when this photograph was taken, the Sheriff was Councillor E.A. Smewin.

The Sheriff usually holds a special breakfast attended by his or her friends and those who have helped to conduct the Drive. People who have no rights of pasture are fined before their beasts can be released to them.

Horses being rounded up on the meadow during the Sheriff's Drive of 1973. The rider in the foreground is Miss Pat Halliday, owner of stables at Hinksey, who for many years helped with the drive and gave lessons to those sheriffs who wished to ride the Meadow but were in need of tuition. In recent years, Sheriffs have conducted the Drive on foot. (Courtesy Oxford Mail and Times.)

Another tradition is the annual inspection of the Common and Meadow by the Sheriff, usually followed by refreshments. For many years an Aunt Sally match was held with the Freemen competing against the Sheriff's team. This is a traditional Oxfordshire pub garden game in which wooden sticks are thrown at a 'doll' mounted on a poll in an attempt to dislodge it. The photograph shows the winning Sheriff's team on 21st June 1973 at the Red Lion, Wolvercote, after they had beaten the Freemen by 30 dolls to 14. Left to right: Gordon Powell, Bernard Wyatt, Ray Venney (holding the sticks) Hazel Rankin, Mr Oswin (Chairman of the Freemen), Coun. Ann Spokes (Sheriff), Mary Tullo, Coun. John Baker, Coun. Dennis Dyer, Richard Rivers. The doll, decorated and mounted (on poll in front) was larger than usual.

The Sheriff of the City of Oxford holds office for one year and during his or her term takes a special interest in Wolvercote Common and Port Meadow, being Conservator of that expanse of land, unploughed since time immemorial. The Sheriff usually attends the open meetings of the Wolvercote Commoners which are held twice each year.

Whit Monday

Whit Monday was once a big day in the life of Wolvercote and for much of the 19th century and well into the 20th, the ancient Order of Foresters held their festival on that day, together with a church service, entertainment and sometimes a cricket match and a dinner. The Wolvercote Court of Fair Rosamund's Bower was strong in the village and would process through it, the officers carrying banners, and ending up at the Red Lion where they had their clubhouse. All the public houses were open for the whole day on Whit Monday.

The photograph shows the Juvenile (section) of the Foresters, the Oxford Society of which was formed in 1882. One of the senior officers is seen on the right of the picture and there is a banner at the rear. Foresters were part of the Friendly Society movement which ran insurance schemes, providing benefits in case of sickness, infirmity or death and based themselves on a mixture of ritual and benevolence.

The Wolvercote Horticultural Society

The Wolvercote Horticultural Society is one of the most enterprising organisations in Wolvercote and holds three shows a year, usually at the village hall. It has been in existence under this name since 1950 but in earlier times it was joined with Summertown and ran shows and sports at least as far back as 1909.

The committee in about 1950. Left to right: D. Williams, R. Bridges (Vice-President), A. Stringer, G. Tuckwell, R. Bateman, J. Phillips, J. Drewitt, P. Tollett, F. Aries, R. Edwards, E. Stone.

Michael Ledger receiving the Ann Spokes Symonds Cup for photography from Ron Bateman at the Spring Show in 1997 with the Chairman, Mrs R. Barber, looking on.

Classes at the various shows include flowers, floral art, fruit, vegetables, pot plants, cookery, home-made wine, preserves, handicrafts, photography and children's classes. Cups are awarded to the winners of each class.

Ron Bateman, MBE (centre), President of the Wolvercote Horticultural Society and an exhibitor for nearly half a century, with (left) Mollie Harris (local writer and actress who for many years played the part of Martha in the radio serial The Archers) and (right) Councillor Mrs. Queenie Whorley (later Mrs Comfort) when she was Lord Mayor of Oxford. She represented Wolvercote on both City and County Councils. The event was an Oxford in Bloom prizegiving on 6th September 1988. Mr Bateman is one of Wolvercote's best-known personalities and he has chaired the Wolvercote Commoners' Committee for nearly 28 years.

The Great Flood

Wolvercote was no stranger to floods and from the earliest times folk used boats to get about among the low islands. The first vehicle was probably the trunk of a tree hollowed out and propelled by a wooden paddle.

Every winter the houses at the end of Elmthorpe Road were inundated except for Bob Allen's who had wisely built his house above flood level. The annual threat of floods was the reason the church and school, for instance, were built on higher ground to the east. Water used to pour across the fields where Rosamund Road is now, finding its way to Port Meadow. For some weeks in winter the Meadow water freezes over making it, even today, popular for skating and sliding. Wolvercote was jokingly called 'Wapping in the mud.' It is said that it was the might of Father Thames and its floods that saved the Meadow from enclosure. Fords across the river, where Wolvercote bridges are now, were of a very early date and tracks to and from them were our first roads and even the origin of the village.

It is, however, the great flood of 1947 which beats all before and since. From the end of January to mid-March that year all the ground and the snow above it was frozen solid and when the thaw came only the upper layers melted and the water could not penetrate below the deeper layers. Water was thigh-deep in places. Along the side of Rosamund Road planks were placed on piles of bricks so that people could get out to work and to the shops. Mr Bert Wilkins, who died recently at the age of 84, kept pigs at the bottom of his garden in that road and by the Sunday night, when water was half-way up the fencing, he carried five large pigs, one by one, on his shoulders along the planks to reach Allen's yard in Godstow Road. The planks were slippery and walking the plank hazardous but with both hands needed for holding the pigs on his back it was a difficult but successful task.

Mrs Ody, who still lives in Rosamund Road, tells me that she and Mrs Bateman opposite, who also still lives there, were both expecting babies at the time and she decided to leave her home in order to stay with relatives. Both of them asked to be given a lift in the Corporation lorry and asked it they could sit up front. There was no way that either of them, in their condition, could clamber up the back of the lorry but they were both refused. Others managed to borrow a punt and travel in that. There was a funeral at the Baptist church on the Saturday and the coffin was taken through the floods in the Corporation lorry.

Mrs Lane and her neighbour Mrs Jones in Rosamund Road had to share a pair of Wellington boots between them so that they could venture downstairs to their flooded ground floor rooms. After going upstairs again in the 'wellies' one of them would transfer them one by one on the end of a broomstick, via their front bedroom windows, so that the other one could go down to her flooded lower floor.

The floods did not start subsiding until about ten days after the thaw had set in. Then began the great dry-out and clean-up.

Up and dry in the Corporation cart are (left to right) ?, ?, Joan Ayres, Mrs Allen with Mr Mortimer on his bicycle making their way through the floods in Godstow Road.

Floods by Surman's and the old Co-operative shop in Godstow Road.

Wolvercote Independence

In the summer of 1987, Wolvercote declared Independence and on 29th August barriers were erected at the approaches to the village and 'tolls' collected from passing motorists. £3,000 was raised to help pay for a scanner for children at the John Radcliffe Hospital.

Here volunteers are holding up a motorist at one of the border posts. (Courtesy *Oxford Mail and Times.*)

For 20 years, until they were disbanded in 1995, the Wolvercote Water Rabbits, which initiated Independence Day, raised £50,000 for charity, mainly for hospital equipment. It was founded by a group of customers at the Red Lion, which became known to members as 'The Warren', and later switched to The Plough when its landlord became chairman.

Name _____

Address _____

_____

_____

Nationality _____

OFFICIAL STAMP

WOLVERCOTE
BORDER POST

DATE _____

REASON FOR ENTRY

NON RESIDENTS SHALL NOT
WORK OR LIVE IN WOLVERCOTE
UNLESS THEY BUY US
ALL A PINT FIRST

INDEPENDENCE CELEBRATIONS
'WHAT'S ON'

Saturday, August 29th

0700–1200	Wolvercote Fishing Competition
0930	Borders closed and Customs manned
1100	Declaration of Independence Parade
	Flag Ceremony
1200	Pram Race
1300–1500	Races for the younger generation
1500–	Wolvercote Tug of War Competition
1600–2200	National Arts Festival of Wolvercote

Plus – all day Fair, BBQ, games for all, side
shows, and much, much more
– Early rounds of Aunt Sally competition
– Early rounds of Darts competition

Sunday, August 30th

1000–1230	Fun Runs for juniors, seniors and others (!)
1200–1400	Pet show
1300–1400	Events for the disabled
1400–1800	Talent Show and Senior Citizen entertainment and Tea
1800	Hymn Sing with the Baptist Chapel – All welcome
1900 on	Feast of Ulfgar (Roast)

Plus – all day Fair, BBQ, games for all, side
shows, and much, much more
– Aunt Sally World Cup Final
– Darts Final

The passport which was issued on receipt of a donation for the privilege of entering the village.

Wolvercote in Wartime

During the First World War (1914–18), Wolvercote was home to the Flying Corps and the Royal Artillery some of whom were billeted round the village while others were camped on the Meadow. The Russians camped near Godstow Nunnery and the Americans by Second Turn (now Godstow Road). The soldiers kept their guns and carriages near The Plough and practised on the Green before being sent, trained, to France. About 25 were billeted at Lower Farm, having brought their own blankets and straw mattresses but were fed by the farm. Their horses were kept at Manor Farm where five vets attended any sick ones. The Meadow was used as a flying strip, not without sad accidents and consequent burials at the Cemetery.

The photograph shows the Camp and Aerodrome of the Flying Corps, which by then had been renamed the Royal Air Force, on the Meadow in 1918.

By the end of the war many Wolvercote girls had married soldiers or members of the American Air Force. Of the Wolvercote men who served in the War, 33 had the name of Collett and happily all returned. Others were not so lucky and their names are recorded on the War Memorial in St Peter's churchyard. Accompanying the inscription 'To the glory of God and in Memory of the Men of Wolvercote who nobly gave their lives for their country in the Great War 1914—18' are listed 52 names. They are: George Frederick Bayliss, Arthur Burden, Frederick Carter, Alfred Champ, Joseph Sidney Champ, Augustus Cheshire, Richard Claridge, Richard T. Claridge, Sidney Claridge, Arthur Clements, James Cooper, Edmund Cox, Solomon Cox, James William Crook, Walter Cummings, Henry Drewitt, George Freeman, Percy Freeman, Sidney Gardiner, Jesse Gulliver, Fred Hastings, Percy Francis Hedges, Henry Higgs, Walter Howard, Lewis Hunt, Fred Hutt, Victor J. Hutt, William R. Hutt, John William Ley, Albert Loveridge, George Loveridge, Thomas Loveridge, Ernest Mapson, Cecil Merrilees, Edward Millar, James Mitchell, Alfred Morgan, Henry Partridge, Harold Powell, Owen Price, William Rowland, Percy Tollett, Charles Tovey, Frederick Gulliver, Stanley Truby, Bert Waine, Frank Waine, Walter Waine, Sidney Stratton Walker, Abel Frederick Warmington, Charles Wickson, James Woodward.

Mrs Esther Cox (mother of Beulah Loveridge), when recently widowed and needing money, went to work at Alden's farm and during her first Christmas there she cooked for 15 officers.

During the Second World War the Army took over the Meadow again but just for three months after the fall of Dunkirk in 1940. Hundreds of soldiers marched wearily from Cowley barracks to rest on Port Meadow where local residents welcomed them and set up tables and chairs, providing teas and popular songs on gramophones. Peggy Godwin remembers her parents putting up an awning at the back of their stables ('Highbury') adjoining the common under which cups of tea, eggs and chips were served to the soldiers. The ground was covered with camouflaged tents and rows of concrete posts (looking rather like a cemetery), placed there to hinder any possible air landings by invaders.

Many exercises and mock battles took place on the Meadow throughout the war and on one occasion there were pontoon bridges over the river. During one training event the men were living on iron rations which gave an excuse for constant requests for fresh bread. One Women's Institute member had a car-load of men camping behind her garden asking for a bath 'though they were supposed to be dead.'

Oxford was fortunate to escape bombing raids although air raid shelters had been erected. One had mistakenly been put up near Wren's pond and when, inevitably the water rose, it soon became a popular 'swimming bath'. Children collected money in order to send parcels to serving soldiers or prisoners of war. The siren at the Woodstock Road roundabout became quite a member of the community, warning of impending air raids. Mrs Frewin, Women's Insitute President in 1939—41, recalled that the first time it sounded during a W.I. meeting the 'members evaporated' and she was left to close the meeting herself. Many remember the ringing of the church bells in 1940 when invasion was expected. They were then silent until 10th November 1942 when they rang for the 8th Army victory in North Africa.

There were 25 Wolvercote men killed in the war and of these 14 came from the newer part of the parish. The upper and lower villages had remarkably few casualties.

Wolvercote Home Guard ('Dad's Army') in World War II (taken at the St Edward's School boathouse, Godstow). Back row (left to right): Alf Robinson, ?, Fred Malin, Mr Churchhouse, John Hewlett, Mr Humphries, ? 4th row: ?, Mr Millard, Mr − Fitzgerald, Mr Towersey, ?, Mr − Fitzgerald, ?, Roger Walker. 3rd row: ?, ?, Bert Allen, George Bidmead, Mr Nevin, Stan Payne, ?, ?, Simeon Savage, Val Mapson (standing slighty behind), ?. 2nd row: Tom Green, Mr Crosier, Ted Churchhouse, ?, ?, ?, Alf Gomm (with cup) Wilf Godwin. Front row: Alec Stone, ?, Mr Neal, ?, Ernie Loveridge, Harry Drewett, Mr − Churchhouse, Mr Nesbitt (in glasses).

Air Raid Wardens and messenger in World War II. This was the Wolvercote and Upper Wolvercote (D 4) post. Taken in 'The Croft', now Sheriff's Drive, about 1941. Back row: Mr Levant-Struth, ?, ?, ?, Mr Symonds, Ken White, Mr Halsey. 3rd row: ?, ?, ?, Mr Robinson, Mr Diddams, ?, ?, ?, ?, Miss Alden (on the far right; she lived at 'The Croft'). 2nd row: ?, Mr George, Mr Ayres, ?, ?, Mr Heading, Mr A.L.P. Norrington (later Sir Arthur and one-time Vice-Chancellor of Oxford University), Mr Harrison, Mr Drinkwater. Front row: ?, ?, George Cummings, ?, Ray Venney.

Evacuees

On 1st and 2nd September 1939, about 400 London children arrived in Wolvercote from Poplar and West Ham. The schools were Dingle Lane Infants, Junior and Mixed, and part of Frederick Road Senior Girls. The following day came the mothers and babies, who were much harder to find homes for, but most of them returned to London after a few weeks in any case.

Peggy Godwin remembers a Mrs Morgan from Poplar standing with a group of about 50 children on the corner by Bowles' (now Robinson's) shop and being selected by Wolvercote residents. Peggy, who was serving in the shop, noticed two little girls (cousins, both called Lily Anderson) who were the only ones left. She said: 'Oh, Mum, look at those poor little girls, can't we have them?'. Her mother agreed and so the girls came to live with them. The local children shared their classrooms with the Londoners, working in shifts, until April, 1940 when overflow classes were held in the Baptist Church Hall, the Village Hall and the old school. By September 1942, those who remained were absorbed into Wolvercote School.

After Victory in Europe, VE parties were held. Quite a few of the evacuees were still in Wolvercote.

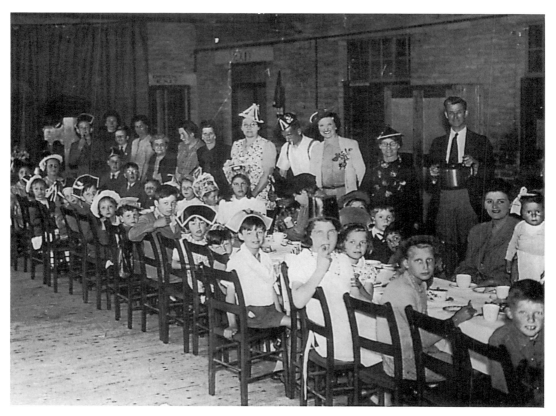

VE Party in the Village Hall in 1945.

VE Party in Elmthorpe Road, 1945. Back row: ?, Mrs Coates, Mrs Eadle, Mrs Thompson, Mrs Butler, Ruby Lovegrove, Jean Hayes, Joan Belcher, Mrs Walker, Mrs Belcher, ?, Mr Allen, ?, Mrs Allen, ?, Elsie Symonds, Bertie Drewett, Mr Eadle, Mr Coates. In the far back, on the right, is Mrs Tipton and, far right, Mrs Waine. Front row: on the left, Betty Coates and Mrs Weaver (holding baby). Others are unidentified.

The Royal British Legion

There has been a British Legion in Wolvercote for over 70 years and their premises are situated off Ulfgar Road, Upper Wolvercote.

The founder of the Legion in Wolvercote was Mr A.F. Parsons who ran the Branch and the Poppy Appeals until he joined the Navy at the start of the Second World War in 1939, serving until 1945.

The Branch was not re-established until 1956. After being housed in various temporary buildings, including a Nissen hut bought from the American forces, the club was finally able to erect the present concrete and brick permanent structure in 1982.

Standard Bearers: Mrs Div Truby of the Women's Section and Mr Niel Johnson.

Fifty years on from VE Day, in 1995, a bonfire was lit on the Green near the Plough. Many Wolvercote people attended and, with the standard bearers from Wolvercote branch of the Royal British Legion, remembered the dead of both World Wars.

Godstow

The main claim to fame of Godstow, or place of God, was its Benedictine Nunnery founded in about 1133 and built on a gravel bank between two streams of the Thames. After its destruction at the Dissolution the site of the Nunnery, or Abbey as it was often called, was given to George Owen, physician to Henry VIII, who converted the buildings into a house. He sold it in 1616 to Sir John Walter. During the Civil War his son, David Walter, attempted to burn the house down to prevent it falling into the hands of Cromwell's men and from about 1645 onwards it was no more than a ruin with the stones being constantly looted for use in buildings in Wytham and Wolvercote, including the house which became the Trout Inn. Part of the old church tower at the Nunnery, which was still standing in the 18th century, was used in the building of Wytham church.

When Montague Bertie, Earl of Abingdon, became the owner of Godstow in 1702 it became part of the Wytham estate. By 1868, Godstow, together with King's Weir to the north, came into Wolvercote as an 'extra-parochial' place. In 1924, its new owner, Raymond ffennell (see Section Fourteen) gave the site to Oxford University. By the late 1930s Godstow was described by members of Wolvercote Women's Institute as being in a state of degredation, consisting of cow sheds, cattle pens. A stone coffin of one ot the Abbesses was reputed to have been used as a water trough. Several coffins were discovered over the years and in 1944 one was found by children which had a female skeleton inside.

Until the late 1930s the road between Godstow and Wytham, on a slightly different line from the present, was gated so giving opportunities to local people to earn a few pennies (from those in passing carriages and later in motor vehicles) for opening and shutting the gates. In 1910, according to Fred Chamberlain's *Recollections,* each gate was attended by people with a disability. For instance, Tommy Norris, a one-legged man, was at one gate and Rhoda Warmington, who was blind, at another. She was at a disadvantage when coins were thrown on the ground and children pounced on them before she could find them. Mrs Savage had the right idea when she wore a big white apron in which she would catch pennies as they were thrown. The gate between Wytham and Botley was said to be kept by a man who whistled up water voles from the nearby Seacourt stream. In later years the children took over the gate-opening, working in twos or threes. One would hold out a hand for the tip (which they shared) while others would open and shut the gates. Colonel ffennell, who lived at the Abbey, often came along in his carriage pulled by two or three horses and the gate-minder, if a man, would take off his hat or, if a woman, she would curtsey.

Despite its small size and the fact that it is officially in Wolvercote, Godstow has maintained its separate identity. This is possibly because of the importance of its three features, the ruined Nunnery, the lock with the lock-keeper's house and the Trout Inn beside the bridge.

The aerial photograph (D. Wilson collection) shows the lock, lock-keeper's house and garden (bottom left) with the Nunnery ruins (centre) and Godstow bridge in the vicinity of the Trout (top right).

The drawing shows Godstow bridge as it was in about 1859. It was rebuilt in the 1880s.

The Nunnery

The Nunnery, sometimes called an abbey, was founded by Dame Edytha (or Ediva) of Winchester, widow of Sir John Lancelyn, in about 1133. It is said that King Stephen, Queen Matilda and their son Eustace attended the dedication of the church there in about 1138 and it was certainly a royal foundation. Families from other parts of the country, together with many from Oxfordshire, sent their daughters to the Nunnery for their education. It was rather like a finishing school and the young ladies were not kept strictly to the religious life and were allowed to visit the houses of neighbouring gentry. Some girls from poor families were also admitted for their education so that it is possible that some early inhabitants of Wolvercote had some sort of schooling there. Almoners from the Nunnery would be sent out to visit the sick and infirm in the neighbourhood and they would even provide shoes for orphans and 'poor clerks'.

At times in the 14th and 15th centruries there were open scandals and children were born to some of the nuns. One bishop accused the Abbess of 'slackening the reins of chastity'. In 1445 both the Abbess and the Prioress agreed that they were unable to prevent Oxford students entering the premises.

The last Abbess, Katherine Buckley, who was described as a shrewd and worldly-wise woman, did her utmost to resist the royal edict of Dissolution but unfortunately to no avail and it was suppressed in 1540. The Nunnery was ransacked, treasures stolen and many of the buildings demolished.

Godstow Nunnery in 1750.

Ruins of the Nunnery in 1850.

The Nunnery in 1997, showing the only building which remains.

Fair Rosamund

Godstow became famous from the late 12th century onwards because of the association with Fair Rosamund, daughter of Walter Clifford, who was the mistress of Henry II. Very probably she was only about 15 and he still a prince when he first saw her there in about 1150. Godstow was midway between the royal palaces of Woodstock and Beaumont. It was said that she did some beautiful needlework for the parish church while she was at Godstow.

After bearing the King two sons, Rosamund died young in about 1176 but it is only a myth that it was at the hands of the jealous Queen Eleanor (Elinor). She is said to have died from natural causes at Woodstock in a spacious apartment or bower which, according to legend, Henry II had made in the shape of a labyrinth. After her death Henry erected a magnificent tomb for her in the Abbey at Godstow and her shrine was obviously much revered. Her father, Walter Clifford, was a benefactor of Godstow and he and his wife were also buried there. The 18th century diarist Thomas Hearne records that the tomb was decorated with 'all sorts of champions and all kinds of animals done to the best advantage.' However, Hugh, Bishop of Lincoln, did not approve and on a visit there in 1194 ordered its removal. It is thought that its new site was in the nuns' chapel which, although destroyed at the Dissolution, has some of its walls still standing. A hazel tree on the site of her tomb was said to have produced nuts with no kernels and was the subject of a sonnet by Robert Southey.

The drawing of King Henry II and Fair Rosamund in 1160 is based on a painting done at the time of the Oxford pageant of 1907.

The Trout

No pub in the area has quite achieved the popularity of the Trout. The house on the site was probably built in the 17th century and in the 18th century the pub had the name 'Godstow House'. Before that it is likely that there was a cottage there belonging to the fish weir keeper. Nets were put across the weir under the bridge which was one of the 'flash locks' used to raise the shallow water to allow barges to come and go, delivering their goods to the Nunnery and other places. Anthony Wood, the Oxford diarist, records a visit to a Godstow alehouse in the 1660s and 1670s. The pub was probably in existence as early as 1625 when the Mayor of Oxford and his party lunched there on their way round the City franchises.

By 1737 it had been almost entirely rebuilt by the tenant, Jeremiah Bishop, known as 'Old Jerry'. At his death in 1771 it is said that he had been 'well-known to most of the gentlemen who have been members of the University within the last 50 years'. Through the centuries the Trout has been a popular place for undergraduates and still is today. In the mid-19th century William Lipscomb was the innkeeeper.

The pub now has a Morse bar named after the famous Inspector Morse, created by the author Colin Dexter, who enjoyed his visits to the Trout.

The photograph shows the Trout and Godstow bridge in about 1880 (D.Wilson collection).

Two photographs taken in about 1905 (D.Wilson collection), showing the terrace and (below) the timber bridge in the Chinese style. This bridge, listed of architectural and historic interest, connected the pub terrace to the island. Although it is now in a ruinous state it looks spectacular when floodlit at night above the rushing stream.

The Trout and weir from the garden on the island in about 1910.

The Mayoral party in August 1931 on their visit after a tour of the City franchises. In the centre of the group next to the Mayor is Mrs Coleman, the licensee of the Trout. On the far right next to the Sheriff is Mr H.O. King of Wolvercote. Mrs Coleman was a great character and a keen swimmer. Leslie Collett of Wolvercote who, at the time, lived in an old bus opposite the pub, used to go swimming in the fast-running stream and he was often joined by Mrs Coleman. Harry Rathband of Wolvercote even remembers swimming with her on her 80th birthday. They swam by the timber bridge. Harry also remembers surface-diving for glasses at the bottom of the stream, not an easy task as the water runs so swiftly there. One afternoon he handed up 60 glasses to a friend in a punt above him. They were mainly pint mugs (tankards and tumblers) which undergraduates had tried to throw across to the island but which had not made it. Harry explains that many of the young men did not realise one had to throw them bottom end first so the air would not come in and impede the glass in flight. He says all the glasses needed washing in acid before they could be used again.

Godstow Lock

Before the days of the lock the barges plied the river carrying goods. They were able to negotiate the shallows because of a series of 'flash locks', one of which was under Godstow bridge and a further one to the north at King's Weir.

The first lock was opened in 1790 and it has been restored on several occasions.

The lock in 1870. At the time canals were made, a pound lock was built which replaced the old flash lock. In 1885 the lock-cut was widened and a relief weir put in which split the island in two. (D. Wilson collection).

The administration of the Thames now comes under the Environment Agency and the lock and weir keeper makes sure that the bylaws regulating the lock are complied with. There are virtually no commercial boats today but the lock is still a busy place with pleasure boats coming and going, especially in the warmer months. About 10,000 come through the lock every year and the lock staff control the river levels.

The lock and weir keeper, David Wilson, on the right, with Andy Whitehead, boatman to the Environment Agency, in the summer of 1996. Along the whole length of the lock is a magnificent display of dahlias which is the work of David Wilson. He has made a special study of the area and has written a short history of Godstow and the Thames.

Wytham

The name, meaning the dwelling at the bend of the river, has existed since at least 968 when King Edgar gave some of its land to Abingdon Abbey. One of the most attractive villages in Oxfordshire, it was, until the 1974 boundary changes, in the County of Berkshire.

Unlike Wolvercote, much of which has become a suburb of the City of Oxford, Wytham's more isolated position at the foot of great Wytham wood, has saved it from ribbon or urban development. Another reason for its picturesque unity has been the fact that, apart from the Church, the Rectory and one or two houses, the whole place has been in the hands of one landowner. Until the University of Oxford took it over, the Lord of the Manor owned and usually lived at Wytham Abbey. The house, never actually an Abbey, was the seat of the Earls of Abingdon until, in 1920, it was sold to Raymond ffennell. The early tenants of the Abbey performed 'knight service' for the King. In time they settled in the village, building a church there, providing a priest, and handing the land down from one generation to another.

Despite the ffennells having put basic electricity in the cottages and modernised half of them, it was said that when the University took it over, every roof leaked. In 1969, in a report commissioned by the University, there were proposals for infilling and extensive modernisation. Fortunately, the voice of conservation prevailed and the 17th and 18th century houses, with their attractive roofs of slate or thatch, and the mellow stone walls which line many of the properties, have been sensitively maintained and 'modernisation' has not involved destruction.

Wytham has not only kept its charm but also some delightful place names such as The Pasticks, Cowleaze Copse, Froghole Cottage, Pibbly Firland, the Bowling Alley and the Singing Way. Some of the old traditional phrases are used by Wytham people even today and one might hear someone asking 'How be?' and be answered by 'very middling thankee'. 'Unked' means 'not well', 'deedily' is 'carefully' and 'spadgers' are 'sparrows'.

Until the First World War, Wytham was famous for its strawberry teas and these were well-patronised by Oxford people. They were eaten in arbours in people's gardens, sitting on stools at roughly-made wooden tables. Each person was allowed half a pound of stawberries at two shillings and sixpence a pound and they were mashed with a port-wine glass before the sugar and cream were added.

The centre of the village is the square formed by the White Hart, Dower House and the Post Office. Children had the roads to themselves until well into the 1930s with nothing more than the odd waggon or dung-cart to disturb them. They would play rounders outside the White Hart, with a look-out at the blind bend, or they would bowl their hoops (iron ones for boys and wooden for girls). In summer, favourite pursuits were fishing or bird-nesting by the Seacourt stream.

Since the University of Oxford acquired the woodlands in 1943 under a deed of covenant with the then owner, Raymond ffennell, they have been intensively studied and researched. There are some long-running studies, started over 50 years ago, one concerning the great tit and another voles and wood mice. In more recent times, there have been experimental programmes connected with environmental change, bringing researchers from other institutions. Because the woods are well-managed and typical of many in this country they are of particular importance for ecologists. The wood-covered heights of Wytham, described by ffennell as the sacred hills, can be seen and appreciated for miles around and give constant pleasure to many who have never visited them.

The present-day adult population of Wytham numbers about 100. The Abbey, which for over thirty years was divided into flats, is once more in private hands. It is now the home of Mr and Mrs Michael Stewart.

The montage picture (courtesy of Oxford University) shows five of the children who were attending Wytham school in 1969. Left to right: Tom Britten, Ian Donaldson, Helen Norman, Christopher Leggett and Jesse Glen. Among the scenes is the dovecote (top centre) which dates from the early 17th century and which now stands in isolation in the middle of the car park of the White Hart. There are no more doves. The bottom of the picture shows, on the left, Mr James Beisley shouldering his axe; middle, the centre of the village with the War Memorial in the distance; right, cows being driven home for milking. At the top left is a wire-scape of aerials and below that an old piece of furniture from the school.

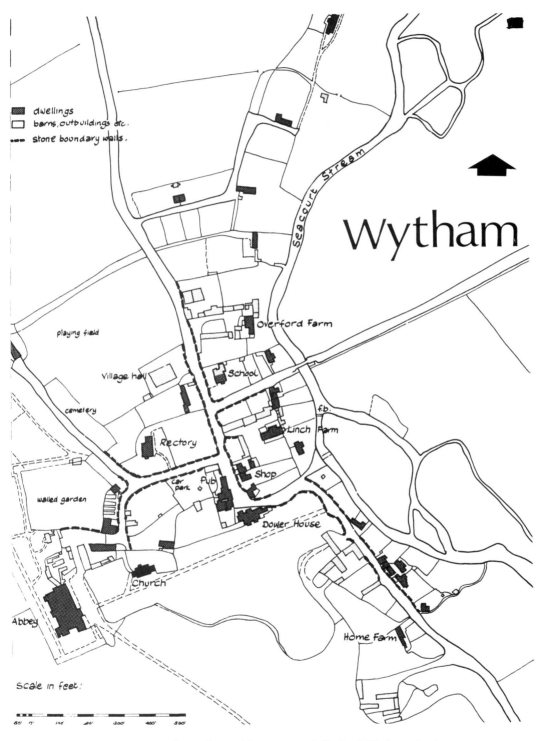

dwellings
barns, outbuildings etc.
stone boundary walls.

Seacourt Stream

Wytham

playing field

Overford Farm

Village hall

School

cemetery

f.b.

Rectory

Linch Farm

walled garden

car park

Pub

Shop

Dower House

Church

Abbey

Home Farm

scale in feet:

50' 0'   100'   200'   300'   400'   500'

1969 map of Wytham. (Courtesy of Oxford University.)

This aerial view (courtesy of M. Clack and Will Soanes) was taken in 1994 from a small balloon and shows Wytham looking south. In the bottom left-hand corner is the road to Godstow and Wolvercote and in the middle to Botley and Oxford. Note the three blind bends. In the distance is the Seacourt stream and beyond (crossing the picture) the A34 by-pass. In the left foreground are the restored

buildings (now houses) of Linch Farm. In the right-hand bottom corner is the dovecote with (to the left) the White Hart Inn across the road from which is the Post Office. The Church and Abbey are to the right out of the picture. The road seen in the bottom left of the picture leads to the old school and village hall.

The School

Wytham had its own school for just over a century, from 1858 to 1969. Now only the buildings remain, both the school and the schoolhouse (where the teacher lived) having been converted into private homes. The old school still has the high windows which let in the light but prevented the children from looking out and being distracted. The school was first endowed by the Dowager Countess Waldegrave and later by Mrs Hope ffennell of Wytham Abbey. When the school was closed the money from its sale was put into the Hope ffennell Trust. The six trustees decide how annual grants should be made, such as books or for learning a trade, and is available for young people up to the age of 25.

In the early part of the century the children would go to school at about five years of age. Boys would be released at the age of 12 to work with their fathers on the farms and the girls left at about 14 often for domestic service, probably in Oxford. In the 1930s the boys would usually stay on until 14 too. Miss Francis Davis was the Head Teacher then and taught the Seniors and Miss White looked after the Juniors. By 1969, the last year of the school's life, there were only nine children attending.

The Old School House, built in 1855, as it is today. It incorporates part of the old school building the back door of which was where the boys entered. The girls came in at the front.

The Old School, with the Old Schoolhouse on the right, taken in 1997.

Wytham children on the radio in 1961. Eric Sims of the BBC interviewing 11-year-old Andrew Dawson for a nature programme. Tenley Soanes is standing behind him on his left. The children had won a BBC Schools Competition with a report on the sparrows in Wytham woods. (Courtesy of *Oxford Mail and Times.*)

The Abbey

The Abbey, though the most important domestic building in Wytham, is because of its isolation behind high walls and trees, detached physically as well as socially. It would have been easy for its owners to cut themselves off from village life. However, even in the days of the Earls of Abingdon, when they resided at the Abbey, they would see that, for instance, the villagers would receive a share of an estate bullock at Christmas time.

It is recorded in George Valentine Cox's *Recollections of Oxford* that, in November 1832, the Duchess of Kent and her daughter stayed with the Earl of Abingdon at the Abbey. Queen Victoria, as the daughter later became, was then 14 years old.

Robert King, who became Steward to the Earls of Abingdon at the age of 25, a position he held from 1816 to about 1841. On the right is his wife Susanna. They lived at the Dower House and it is said that he never overlooked the industrious and deserving. He was one of the earliest promoters of the Royal Agricultural Society and one of the originators of monthly cattle markets. He was in favour of tenants having moderate-sized holdings with good cottages and gardens.

After he left the Abbey, Robert King took up business in George Street, Oxford and the Canal Wharf nearby. He retired to West Lawn, Kidlington. He died in 1870 at the age of 79 and both he and Susanna are buried in Kidlington churchyard.

The Abbey as it is today. The exterior is much the same as it was when Montague Bertie, 5th Earl of Abingdon, rebuilt the old house in 1812. There has probably been a house on the site since the 12th century when the manor was held by a family called de Wytham. It then passed to Sir Richard Harcourt who, in the 16th century, sold it to Lord Williams of Thame. After his daughter, Margery, wife of Henry Norris, died it went through the female line to the Bertie's when Bridget, Baroness Norris, married Montague Bertie.

In the 16th century the building consisted of two adjoining quadrangles but it was so altered early in the 19th century that the original arrangement is hard to define exactly. The south courtyard was built over and an entrance hall and a great staircase created. The windows in the north range are, in part, old and the west range of the north courtyard is partly original. The south side was entirely refaced. The old servants hall on the north side of the north quadrangle is part of the original building.

The entrance to the gateway tower of the Abbey (from the east).

The Abbey, south front and garden, 1996.

The Abbey, west front 1996.

The ffennells

Raymond ffennell (1871–1944) and his wife Hope (1878–1956) and their only child Hazel (1905–1939) came to Wytham during the First World War from South Africa. Because they could not buy the Abbey until 1920 they camped in great style in the wood.

Raymond ffennell, sometimes called Colonel, with the Abbey depicted in the background. He was a member of the Senior Common Room of New College. The ffennells participated in village life and it was thanks to their daughter Hazel that there was considerable communication between the tenants and the family of the Lord of the Manor. At Christmastime, for instance, 10 cwt. of coal was delivered to every household. The whole school was taken to the Pantomime in Oxford, kindness of the ffennells, and an annual Christmas tea party was held at the Abbey with every child being given a big present. Another party was held at the Village Hall, a building which had been given by Mrs ffennell.

The Village Hall viewed from the rear in 1997. It was designed like a woodland chalet.

Apart from Christmas, there were also parties at other times: a primrose party when all went to the wood to pick the flowers, returning afterwards to the Abbey; a gravel party, when the children went to the Abbey to rake the gravel in the animal runs, and the blackberry party which was held after blackberry-picking in the woods. No child wanted to miss these parties. On Hazel ffennell's birthday in July she would always visit the village school where each child would give her a small bunch of flowers and, rather like today's royalty, her lady's maid would carry them back. People 'knew their place' in those days and if any child saw a member of the ffennell family they had to curtsy (if a girl) or salute (if a boy). A lady who grew up in Wytham, remembers that Mrs ffennell asked her a question at the Christmas Party and she replied 'Yes, Miss'. She was rebuked by Mrs ffennell who pointed out: 'Miss Hazel is Miss and I am Madam'! Children would take such a telling off in their stride and readily admitted their mistakes. On the other hand, the ffennells were good to individuals who needed help. For example, Mrs ffennell provided a car to take a mother to the hospital for check-ups when she was expecting twins, but people kept quiet about receiving help.

Shoots would take place in the woods in season and people from Wolvercote as well as Wytham would come to help as gunloaders, beaters or as 'stops' to prevent the birds flying out of the woods. At the end of the day parties of Wolvercote pensioners would be picked up by the 'toffs' who would drive them to receive their money.

During the Second World War the Abbey was home to four London evacuees from Poplar for whom it was quite a culture shock. Some of them had never slept in sheets before. The ffennels were then still suffering from the loss of Hazel and saw little of the four Burns boys. However, they were well cared for with the run of the Estate and a chance to see Hazel's animals and performing birds. After a while, Colonel ffennell came to befriend them and taught the two elder boys to shoot and jujitsu. They were driven in a Daimler to have their hair cut and they felt like Little Lord Fauntelroys. The Colonel was not to see the end of the war, dying in 1944, and on Mrs ffennell's death in 1956 the Abbey became the property of the University. By then, the Abbey was falling into disrepair with leaking roofs and doves flying around inside.

Hazel ffennell

If Fair Rosamund is the folk heroine of Godstow Hazel ffennell could be said to be the same for Wytham.Those still living there who knew her confirm that she was popular, naturally friendly and had no enemies. Said to have an immense capacity for genuine enjoyment, she radiated a perpetual happiness for others. All animals were her friends and she had a special gift of communicating with them. She was also an accomplished artist, linguist, modeller and dancer. A talented and born producer of plays and films, she at first encouraged the young village men to play in her mouth-organ band.

Hazel (centre) with her mouth-organ band of Wytham men, founded in 1933.

Then she started the Wytham Wonders, later to become the Wytham Players, whose theatrical performances she produced with a cast entirely of Wytham people. Proceeds went to charity. It is said that she could take any part herself and showed each actor what she wanted. As others have since discovered, Wytham is an ideal place for film work.

Hazel also told fortunes at fêtes and charity balls and was able to pass herself off as a Spanish gypsy. On one occasion at a stately home she played the part so well that she was ordered by a waiter to have her meal with the kitchen staff. She once made a film of Cinderella with all 17 parts played by 7 diffferent types of pigeon and she would often be seen with her favourite dove Julia on her shoulder. For some years she had tame meercats, one of whom, called Rikki, met the King.

Tragically, Hazel died after a long and painful illness, lasting some years, at the early age of 33. The big iron gates at the access from the road to the Abbey drive were shut on her death in 1939 and not opened again for over 50 years. The main portion of the 960 acres of Wytham woodlands, on their transfer to the University in 1943, were called the 'Woods of Hazel' as a permanent memorial to her. She is buried, as are her parents, in Wytham churchyard.

*'It is difficult to understand why such a beautiful life
should have been cut short so soon but perhaps one
day a legend will grow up around the grave at Wytham
as treasured as that of Fair Rosamund who was laid to
rest in the nearby Nunnery at Godstow.'*

Mostyn Davies (Major DSO) 1940.

Hazel on Buallog, one of the Guernsey cows which supplied all the milk, butter and cheese for the Abbey.

King George V meets Hazel ffennell's meercat at a review of cadets in the Parks in Oxford in about 1915 when Hazel was ll years old. Having met the king, Hazel drew a picture of Rikki with a crown upon his head. In this photograph, Hazel has a motoring veil over her head.

Rikki.

Rikki crowned.

Portrait of Hazel, with her favourite dove, painted by Harold Speed in the late 1920s or early 1930s.

Drawing of the memorial window to Hazel ffennell which was once in the Church but which fell into disrepair and was destroyed. It shows some of her animals and birds, including her dogs, Flick and Floss, and the front of the Abbey.

The Country Schools, now Hill End Camp

One of the requirements for treating tuberculosis (TB), the often fatal disease, was fresh air. Colonel Raymond ffennell of Wytham Abbey, having plenty of that commodity, devised a scheme to bring children from the towns, where the death rate from TB was highest, into the country. He started open-air schools on his land so that not only delicate children but whole classes could come with their teachers thus not interrupting the curriculum. His so-called 'country schools' started in 1931 with brick-built classrooms and 'water-borne' sanitary arrangements. The fireplaces could take wood or coal, making them suitable for year-round use. In the first year 500 children had paid a weekly visit and it was so successful, especially for children's health, that by 1932 as many as 300 children came daily. Not only did the children get fresh air and sunlight but a midday rest on wooden 'reclining boards' and a chance to learn about and appreciate nature. As well as local children, some came from London for a fortnight at a time and stayed in specially-built dormitories. As the schools started at Hill Farm the place came to be known as Hill End.

Will Soanes of Wytham remembers going there for one day a week with their teacher. They took lunch-boxes and learnt about wildlife and nature. The country schools played their part in controlling disease and in 1933, when 15 schools were sending classes, the Medical Officer of Health and the Clinical School Medical Officer for Oxford both issued favourable reports.

In the 1950s Hill End was taken over by Oxford City Council and since 1973 has been run by the County Council. Although TB is now a rare disease children are still benefitting from the open-air facilities and a chance to learn about country life 66 years on. Since 1984 the Camp has been amalgamated with the Field Studies Centre which had been on the site since 1968. Latest figures (for 1995) are 4,000 day visitors a year from 42 different Oxfordshire schools and over 5,000 residential visitors a year from 2,000 different schools all over the country. Mrs Kathy Day, a head teacher who has taken children from several small schools to Hill End, says it is a 'magical place' and especially so because she lives in Wytham. Hill End is such an important experience for children that it is hoped that this priceless asset can remain open for many years to come.

Children with their 'resting-boards in 1932. They could also be used as seats for open-air classes.

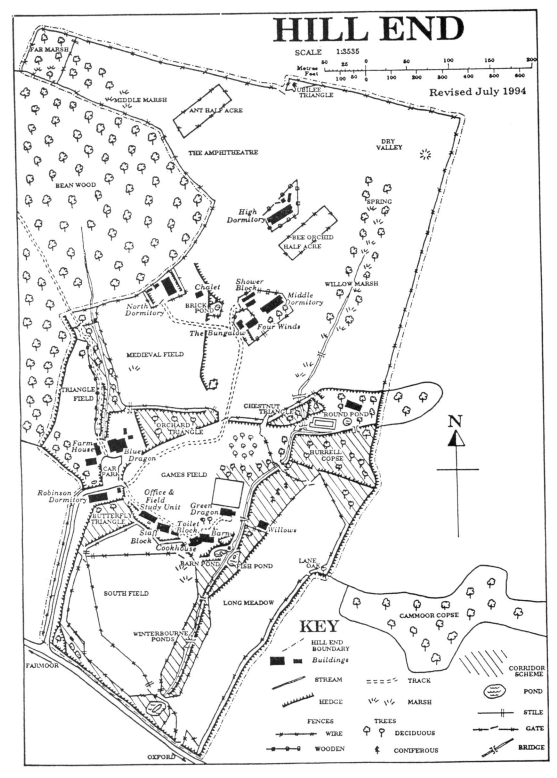

Map of Hill End Camp as it was in 1994.

The joys of Hill End. Running southwards from the Dry Valley in the 1970s.

Recording wildlife at Hill End in one of the classrooms.

Drawings by Vana (courtesy of Hill End).

One of the 1930's buildings at Hill End. It is called the Green Dragon after the dragon bootscraper (seen under the second window from the right), which was designed by Hazel ffennnel. (February 1997.)

One of the original dormitories built in the 1930s for the country schoools. (February 1997.)

All Saints' Church, Wytham

A church existed in the early Norman period but no trace remains and the present church, rebuilt by the Bertie family in 1811-12, was constructed largely of materials brought from Cumnor when their 14th C manor house there was pulled down by the 6th Earl of Abindon. The Berties' owned two manors. Some stones may also have come from Godstow abbey. The 15th C windows of the chancel and the carved corbels in the nave roof, however, belong to the original church. One goes through an unusual 16thC stone gateway to reach the church which is secluded within its walls and surrounded by trees. The gateway was probably brought from Cumnor Place and has the date 1573 carved on the head.

The group is of Wytham Church Choir in about 1930, seated in front of the porch. Back row: (left to right) ?, ?, Bill Girvan, Mr Pratley, Mr Hitchman, Mr Thompson (from Wolvercote), Ted Floyd, Mr Savage (from Wolvercote), ?, Mr Ronnie Barrett, Mr Broadis. Middle row: ?, Mr Soanes, Mr Wilkins, the Reverend Algernon Sidney Mills (Rector), Mr Syd Podbury, Mr Matthews, Mr Chamberlain (from Wolvercote), ?. Front row: Joey Bucknell, Hubert Hardy, John Gurden, Percy Broadis (?), Fred Loveridge, Harold Neale, ?.

The Four Aces and friends. Wytham group of motor-cyclists, July 1955. Back row (left to right): Eddie Warner, John Soanes, an unknown friend. Front row: Ivor Trafford, Will Soanes, Stan Neale.

Reverse Dress Cricket Match, about 1968/69. Left to right: ?, Dave Franklin, Jim Warren, Will Soanes, Tony Wordman, Des Newport, Bob Dawson, Nick Painter, George Thomas, Allen Nightingale. (Courtesy W. Soanes.)

Ladies of the Parents' Association in Wytham preparing the Christmas lunch for older members, 1986. Left to right: Mrs Scott-Taylor, her daughter, Alice, and Mrs Janet Fenton. (Courtesy Mrs Ruth Thomas.)

The White Hart Inn and a traffic problem, 1996. (Courtesy Mrs Ruth Thomas.)

There has been an inn on the site of the White Hart since at least 1726. The name was first recorded in 1854. Halls' Brewery acquired the freehold in 1928, having leased it from 1919. Since 1958 the owners have been what is known today as Allied Domecq Leisure. It is a popular place with locals and visitors alike in every season of the year. Although Wytham was once a quiet and peaceful place, where children could play rounders in the road outside the pub, its main problem today is traffic. It is particularly bad at peak hours when the village is used as a rat-run by motorists trying to avoid hold-ups on the nearby A34.

In the old days Wytham probably looked more like this winter scene of 1985 which shows Mr Dawson gritting the road. (Courtesy Mrs Ruth Thomas.)

Wytham continues to be a popular place for shooting films. In July, 1991, the funeral scenes in The Camomile Lawn by Mary Wesley were filmed at the church, converted into St Buryan's church, St Gothian. The pictures were taken in July, 1991 while waiting for the action to begin. (Courtesy Mrs Ruth Thomas.)

Felicity Kendal with Nicholas Le Prevost.

Claire Bloom, and the actor who played the Vicar, with Virginia MacKenna in the background.

Some of the extras from Wytham and Wolvercote who formed the funeral party. Left to right: ?, Mrs Teresa Brant, ? , Mr Dawson (with umbrella), ?, Mrs Ruth Thomas.